NEW YORK'S 100

Best
Little
Hotels

THIRD EDITION

ALLEN SPERRY

DRAWINGS BY JOHN COBURN

UNIVERSE
New York

First Published in the United States of America in 2003
by Universe Publishing
a Division of Rizzoli International Publications, Inc.
300 Park Avenue South
New York, NY 10010

Copyright © 1997, 1999, 2003 by Allen Sperry

All rights reserved. No portion of this book may be reproduced,
stored in a retrieval system, or transmitted in any form or by any
means, electric, mechanical, photocopying, recording, or otherwise,
without prior consent of the publishers.

Interior Design: Heather Zschock
Cover Design: Paul Kepple and Jude Buffum @ Headcase Design
Cover Illustration: Mary Lynn Blasutta

Drawings copyright © 1997, 1999 by John Coburn

2003 2004 2005 2006 2007 / 10 9 8 7 6 5 4 3 2 1

Printed in the United States
Third Edition

Library of Congress Control Number: 2002115763
ISBN: 0-7893-0859-2

Publisher's Note:
Neither Universe nor the author has any interest, financial or personal, in the locations listed in this book. No fees were paid or services rendered in exchange for inclusion in these pages. While every
effort was made to ensure that information regarding phone numbers, rates, and services was accurate and up-to-date at the time of
publication, it is always best to call ahead and confirm.

Acknowledgments:
With many thanks to Jill Rabelais for her invaluable assistance and
to John Coburn for his charming drawings and endless enthusiasm.

To Claudia,
Alexandra, and Mark

Contents

Introduction

I like hotels with their own personality, their own sense of style; hotels that reflect the special taste of their owners and the energy and character of their neighborhoods; hotels that offer a unique experience that is unexpected, unforgettable. And I love New York.

I wrote this book for the travelers in search of something different, something special—a hotel, to paraphrase hip hotelier Ian Schrager, that knows its own state of mind. My "little" hotel is a boutique hotel that—no matter its size, architecture, design, décor, staff, or amenities—creates an atmosphere and lodging experience that you can't have anywhere else.

When the first edition of this book was published in 1997, I really had to dig to find 50 hotels that satisfied my criteria. Now, six years later and into our third edition, there are 100 hotels in New York that I would classify as "boutique" and more on the horizon, scheduled to open in the next few years. New York has never had a greater variety of boutique hotels to choose from, which has really worked to the traveler's advantage. There is a wonderful boutique hotel in New York for everyone, no matter his or her budget or disposition.

If you want to be in the center of it all but are on a limited budget, book one of the cheaper rooms at the Habitat, and get change from your $100 bill. For a romantic weekend, book the Cottage Room at the 1871 House on the Upper East Side. The W Times Square and the City Club offer high style and cutting-edge design amidst luxury and comfort, while 60 Thompson and the Tribeca Grand appeal to the creative soul that needs to be downtown to feel at home. And for the adventurous spirit, the quirky French charm of Le Gamin Bed and Breakfast may be just the thing.

As many of New York's smaller hotels have no dining facilities and limited room service, I have included suggestions for nearby restaurants with each entry. These local eateries offer wonderful food that will complement your experience: try the *pollo ex mixote* at Mi Cocina on Jane Street in the Village, sip a Brazilian *caipirinha* at Circus, near Bloomingdale's, or luxuriate over a quiet country brunch of pumpkin waffles and eggs Benedict at Sarabeth's on Madison Avenue. All are landmarks on the City's dining trail.

Finally, in the back section of the book I have included 15 additional hotels that you may want to consider if you are traveling on a more limited budget. Of these, the Urban Jem Guesthouse is of particular note both for the engaging personality of its proprietress, Jane Alex Mendelson, and its location in the Mount Morris Park Historic District of Harlem. Venture out a little and you never know what undiscovered delights you may find.

Whatever your situation, there is a place here that is just right for you. Have a wonderful time.

Allen Sperry
New York City, 2003

Abingdon Guesthouse

13 Eighth Avenue at West 12th Street
Phone: (212) 243-5384 Fax: (212) 807-7473
Number of Rooms: 9
Price Range: Single, $137–$212;
double with private bath, $167–$222
Credit Cards: Most major
www.abingdonguesthouse.com

FINDING THIS PRECIOUS GEM tucked away in the way West Village can be daunting, as there is no sign nor obvious entryway, and the nearby streets eschew numerical simplicity for strange names like Bethune, Gansevoort, and Horatio. But soon you're mounting the steep and narrow but well-tended staircase to the second floor of a West Village townhouse to find yourself in Nantucket or a guest house in the Cotswolds; you are immediately transported from the howls and horns of Eighth Avenue to a set of rooms reminiscent of a cozy country inn. It is no coincidence that the friendly proprietors, Steve and Sass, formerly lived in the leafy splendor of the hills of Washington Depot, Connecticut. Their New England sensibility and eclectic taste pervade every carefully chosen item in these

romantically quirky little B&Bs. Each room in each of two brownstones has its own personality, and even the names— the Perrin Room, the Sherwin Room, the Landau Room— hint at the charms that await you inside.

Oriental carpets adorn the polished hardwood floors. Architectural, animal, and fish prints, along with handwoven baskets and even a Georgia O'Keeffe–like bleached steer skull adorn the freshly painted walls. Thick designer bath towels hang on antique towel racks, and the mantelpieces over the nonworking fireplaces display whimsical collectibles from years of antiquing and flea marketing. There is color everywhere: hunter green, southwestern red, and mauve for the room walls, and a profusion of tones that could have come from Matisse's palette for the bedspreads. Upholstered armchairs with needlepoint pillows complement the four-poster beds. Bathrooms are white-tiled and gleamingly clean, and dressing-room mirrors are encircled by theater bulbs for easier shaving or makeup application.

The lack of any public space and the close proximity of the rooms to each other serve to remind you that you're in New York, where space is a commodity. But you need only head downstairs to the Brewbar Cafe (same owners) for a frothy cappuccino and a tasty pastry to be renewed and ready to explore the nooks, crannies, and hidden mysteries of this historic neighborhood.

GUEST SERVICES: TV; safe in room or on premises; hair dryer; iron and ironing boards.
NEIGHBORHOOD RESTAURANTS: Benny's Burritos, 113 Greenwich Ave. at Jane St., 727-0584 (cheap Mexican fare, funky and popular); Corner Bistro, 331 W. 4th St. at Jane St., 242-9502 (popular local pub for burgers and beer); Florent, 69 Gansevoort St. at Washington St., 989-5779 (24-hour French diner with delicious fare and eclectic hip crowd); Mi Cocina, 57 Jane St. at Hudson St., 627-8273 (inventive Mexican in a light, airy space); White Horse Tavern, 567 Hudson St. at W. 11th St., 989-3956 (landmark Village tavern for beers and burgers).

Algonquin Hotel

59 West 44th Street bet. Fifth and Sixth Avenues
Phone: (212) 840-6800 Fax: (212) 944-1449
Number of Rooms: 165
Price Range: Single, $240; two-bedroom suite, $525
Credit Cards: All major
www.thealgonquin.net

ALTHOUGH MANY STORIES, characters, celebrities, and myths have been associated with the Algonquin over the years, there are two bits of history that particularly sum up what the Algonquin is really all about. One is a quote: "When I was growing up, I had three wishes—I wanted to be a Lindbergh-type hero, learn Chinese, and become a member of the Algonquin Round Table" (John F. Kennedy). The second is the hotel's practice of giving every guest a copy of the most recent *New Yorker* magazine. The Algonquin is about its history, particularly its literary history, as well as its role as a shrine to the heyday of New York culture between the wars. Many books and movies have paid homage to this landmark from *Catcher in the Rye* to the recent *Mrs. Parker and the Vicious Circle*. The notables who have slept, drunk, written, and dined here throughout the past century include some of the most famous names in our theatrical, literary, and cinematic pantheons. The Algonquin has done its best to retain the aura of those times with its oak-paneled Victorian lobby-as-library/lounge, heavy with antique-y furnishings and Oriental carpeting.

The adjoining rooms are hallowed spaces steeped in a history that evoke images of dry martinis, thick cigarette smoke, feather boas, and laughter: the Rose Room (home to the legendary Round Table); the Oak Room (launching platform for the careers of Michael Feinstein and Harry Connick, Jr., among many

THE NEW YORKER
WAS CREATED
UNDER THIS CHANDELIER

others); and the Blue Bar (reputed to serve New York's finest Bloody Mary). These public rooms are a living museum to a way of New York life gone by. A sip of English tea or a Bombay gin highball in the lobby around 6 P.M., as another New York evening unfolds, can almost bring it all back.

Upstairs, this clubby nostalgic New York aesthetic gives way to a more conservative aura. All the rooms are nicely renovated, clean and spacious, decorated with much floral enthusiasm, and eminently livable. Furnishings are classic, conservative reproductions of American and European styles. The signature suites draw on the hotel's history by featuring memorabilia associated with the famous names they've been given: Dorothy Parker, the *New Yorker*, *Vanity Fair*, *Playbill*, Al Hirschfeld, the Algonquin Round Table, and James Thurber.

It is, in some way, ironic that the Royalton stands right across the street from this grand old hotel. The Royalton and its clientele became the '90s version of what the Algonquin used to represent in its heyday—a beacon for the media elite.

If fondness for the past finds you looking back longingly, you're sure to find a sense of contentment, outstanding personal service, and comfort at the Algonquin. And if you're seeking inspiration, you may find it here too. Hey, Alan Jay Lerner wrote *My Fair Lady* in room 908.

GUEST SERVICES: Bar; fitness center; Internet access; laundry service; parking; restaurant; room service; safe in room; TV/VCR; 2-line telephones with data port and voicemail.

NEIGHBORHOOD RESTAURANTS: Cafe Un Deux Trois, 123 W. 44th St., bet. 6th Ave. and Broadway, 354-4148 (large, active French bistro); Carmine's, 200 W. 44th St., 221-3800 (great old-fashioned Italian food; fun and packed); Hamburger Harry's, 145 W. 45th St., bet. 6th Ave. and Broaday, 840-2756 (decent, well-priced burgers).

The Avalon

16 East 32nd Street bet. Fifth and Sixth Avenues
Phone: (212) 299-7000 Fax: (212) 299-7001
Number of Rooms: 100
Price Range: Superior rooms, $199–$350; junior suites,
$270–$450; deluxe suites, $315–$499;
executive suites, $375–$600
Credit Cards: All major
www.theavalonny.com

THIS IS A CITY OF CONTRASTS. In the middle of a bustling Midtown commercial street lined with well-known Korean restaurants sits a serene and sparkling diamond of a hotel: the Avalon. This small, luxurious European-style boutique hotel, catering to business and leisure travelers alike, is right around the corner from the Empire State Building and a few blocks from Madison Square Garden, the Garment Center, and the world's largest department store, Macy's.

From the busy sidewalk you enter a hushed and gleaming neoclassical lobby with sparkling Italian marble floors. This is a hotel that is elegant, serious, and as efficiently run as a leading corporate law firm. It understands your needs and quietly caters to them. But there's also cool jazz on the sound system, and armchairs flanking the Indian butler's coffee table in the library invite you to unwind and relax.

Upstairs the rooms are ultra-quiet, reasonably sized, and very comfortable. They feature the hotel's signature Body Pillows (surely a treat), and brand name amenities like Bose Wave radios and luxurious Frette bathrobes. Bathrooms are a feast of imported Italian marble, mirrors, two-sink vanities, thick towels, and Aveda bath products. The business traveler, especially, will appreciate the state-of-the-art communications systems equipped with every bell and whistle imaginable.

The Avalon marries many of the luxuries and comforts of a big four-star hotel with the intimacy of a boutique hotel. The business traveler and the visitor looking for a small, elegant hotel in Midtown will be exceedingly happy here. A couple of tips when making your reservation: Ask for a room facing the Empire State Building. The view of New York's favorite landmark from the Avalon is one of the best anywhere. And book a table for dinner at The Avalon Bar & Grill, the neighborhood's best American restaurant, located right in the hotel.

GUEST SERVICES: Fitness center nearby; Internet access; restaurant/bar; room service; TV/VCR; valet parking.

NEIGHBORHOOD RESTAURANTS: Meli Melo, 110 Madison Ave. bet. 29th and 30th Sts., 686-5551 (casual French/American bistro; reasonable prices); Park Bistro, 414 Park Avenue South bet. 27th and 28th Sts., 689-1360 (authentic French bistro with excellent food and atmosphere); Artisanal, 2 Park Avenue South at 32nd St. (a cheese-lover's delight); Mosaico, 175 Madison Ave. bet. 33rd and 34th Sts., 213-4700 (inexpensive and inventive nuevo Latino).

Hotel Beacon

2130 Broadway (at 75th Street)
Phone: (212) 787-1100 Fax: (212) 724-0829
Number of Rooms: 222
Price Range: Single, $165; two-bedroom suite, $450
Credit Cards: All major
www.beaconhotel.com

MAYBE IT IS THE OPERA SINGER practicing her scales in the next room, or the group of ballet dancers heading out to rehearsal. Possibly it is the view across the street of the famous Fairway Market and the Citarella fish shop. Or the fact that the park is only two blocks away and Lincoln Center a ten-minute walk. These are the sights and sounds of life in New York. This is what life looks like to a New Yorker living in this part of town.

Situated smack dab in the middle of this thriving Upper West Side residential neighborhood, the Beacon is for those who don't require a lot of luxuries but want a clean, safe place to stay in an area where there is a great deal going on. This is what most New Yorkers ask of their living arrangements, and this is what the Beacon delivers.

Built in 1927, the hotel has undergone a recent renovation. Rooms are large and homey, each with a kitchenette. Don't forget to request a room on one of the higher floors, as many of these look out over the Hudson River and Central Park. (Please note: Most New Yorkers do not have a view like this.) Bathrooms have a prewar spaciousness and feature newly glazed fixtures. Room furnishings are new and conservatively inoffensive (what's not to like in a peachy, flowered bedspread), and everything is meticulously clean. Room service becomes unnecessary when within a few blocks of the hotel there are hundreds of great restaurants, many of which will deliver right to your room.

The lobby is a veritable Tower of Babel with Europeans, South Americans, and Australians intermingling with dance troupes in town for a performance and opera buffs on their way to the Met. Who knows—maybe that voice singing "La donna è mobile" across the hall is the next Pavarotti.

GUEST SERVICES: Fitness center nearby, discounted for hotel guests; kitchen facilities including microwave; safe in room; parking nearby; restaurant; TV.

NEIGHBORHOOD RESTAURANTS: Gray's Papaya, 2090 Broadway at 72nd St., 799-0243 (New York classic; cheap hot dogs and juice); La Caridad, 2199 Broadway at 78th St., 874-2780 (cheap and good; a classic Cubano-Latino joint).

Bed & Breakfast
on Downing Street

30 Downing Street bet. Sixth Avenue and Bedford Street
Phone/Fax: (917) 568-3377
Number of Rooms: 2
Price Range: $120–$150
Credit Cards: None
B&B@legamin.com

RIP OUT THIS PAGE. Don't tell your friends. Keep it to yourself. This is a find. A one-of-a-kind New York experience. Located on a tree-lined, impossible-to-find street in the West Village, this two-room B&B on Downing Street is run by a charming Frenchman who lives upstairs with his wife and child. Part of the group that also includes the downtown cafés Le Gamin-Soho, Le Gamin-Chelsea, and Les Deux Gamins, this is about as low-key and uncommercial as it gets. As they never advertise and are rather casual about whether they get any business or not, it's word-of-mouth recommendations that bring guests to their royal blue door. Not that you will be overwhelmed with conveniences and amenities. Keep in mind, this is just two rooms, each with a private bath. But the whole feeling and experience is so unusual and unlike anything you're likely to find anywhere else in the city that you can't help but be charmed. There's a bit of an "I can't believe I found this place. Isn't it cool" kind of feeling. And the American tendency to be impressed by anything remotely French doesn't hurt either.

Rooms are of average size, but appear recently renovated with new wood floors and exposed brick walls. In one room, the brass bed sports a cozy down comforter, and the old wooden desk with the phone and answering machine looks like a flea market find. Bathrooms are warm and homey with black-and-white tiled floors, gilded mirrors, and a soothing golden yellow paint washed on the walls.

Breakfast is offered in any of Le Gamin's charming nearby cafés, which serve as local commissaries for the hip Euro-crowd and neighborhood artistes.

What is great about this place is that it is so laid-back, so out of the way, so different. Just finding it gives one a sense of discovery and accomplishment. One of the many joys of being in New York is unearthing some little treasure you never knew was here.

GUEST SERVICES: Complimentary breakfast.
NEIGHBORHOOD RESTAURANTS: Jean-Claude, 137 Sullivan St. bet. Prince and Houston Sts., 475-9232 (wonderful, simple contemporary bistro fare at reasonable prices); Trattoria Spaghetto, 232 Bleecker St. at Carmine St., 255-6752 (good cheap Italian); Les Deux Gamins, 170 Waverly Place, 807-7357.

Beekman Tower Hotel

3 Mitchell Place, 49th Street at First Avenue
Phone: (212) 355-7300 Fax: (212) 753-9366
Number of Rooms: 174
Price Range: Studio suite, $368; one-bedroom suite,
$454; two-bedroom suite, $740
Credit Cards: All major
www.mesuite.com

SOARING 26 STORIES OVER BEEKMAN PLACE and the East River, the Beekman Tower Hotel is an art deco landmark located on a cul-de-sac in one of New York's most affluent zip codes. Constructed in 1928, the hotel was completely renovated in 1997 and today evokes the ambiance and grace of a 1930s transatlantic ocean liner. The beautiful lobby is equal to and maybe surpasses anything you will see in the Chrysler or Empire State buildings.

Staying at the Beekman is like having your own apartment in New York. In this full-service hotel, all the guest rooms are bright and spacious suites, and each has a kitchen. Furnishings are traditional, ceilings are high, and amenities are plentiful. If you reserve on an upper floor, request a suite with a terrace—you'll also have a sweeping view of the city and the river.

Tucked against the East River and around the corner from Sutton Place, this pocket of affluence has been home to some of New York's most famous citizens including Irving Berlin and the relatives of the Shah of Iran. The United Nations is just a few blocks to the south and numerous foreign missions and consulates are just minutes away. The staff at the Beekman caters to this diplomatic community (and top-level executives) with the utmost professionalism, warmth, and demonstrable pride in their establishment.

Thanks to the Top of the Tower piano bar on the 26th floor, with its breathtaking wraparound views of the city, the Beekman has traditionally been the best place in the city to go on your first date. It was selected as one of the top ten romantic destinations in *The Best Places to Kiss,* and the Zephyr Grill, off the lobby, with an eclectic continental menu, is perfect for quiet conversation.

While the Beekman is near enough to Midtown and the city's great restaurants, bars, and nightclubs, it is far enough removed so that once back in the hotel, you're ensconced in a hushed world of understated elegance and refinement. It's a taste of old world bliss.

GUEST SERVICES: Fitness center; Internet access; kitchen facilities; minibar; parking; restaurant/bar; room service; safe in room; TV/VCR.

NEIGHBORHOOD RESTAURANTS: Billy's, 948 First Ave. bet. 52nd and 53rd Sts., 355-8920 (classic old New York neighborhood pub with good honest fare); Wylie's Ribs, 891 First Ave. at 50th St., 751-0700 (arguably the best ribs in town); Zephyr Grill, 3 Mitchell Place at 49th St. and 1st Ave., 223-4200 (art deco restaurant in hotel).

The Benjamin

125 East 50th Street (at Lexington Avenue)
Phone: (212) 715-2500 Fax: (212) 715-2525
Number of Rooms: 209
Price Range: Superior guest room, $420; deluxe guest room,
$465; one-bedroom suite, $530; two-bedroom suite, $950
Credit Cards: All major
www.thebenjamin.com

IT IS SAID THAT THE BENJAMIN is where the top diplomats and CEOs go when the Waldorf-Astoria is fully booked. This luxury executive suite hotel opened in April of 1999 after a one-year, $30 million renovation. Formerly the Beverly Hotel, it has been transformed into a majestic and impressive boutique hotel catering to the needs of the modern business and leisure traveler.

Designed by architect Emery Roth of the San Remo, St. Moritz, and Normandy fame, this 30-story building was built in 1927 and features the "wedding cake" style of architecture with inset upper floors that allow balconies and terraces in many of the guest rooms. Renovated in a conservative neoclassical style, the Benjamin is a marriage of old and new, combining the best of the building's former glory with all that modern technology can deliver. While the lobby features soaring ceilings, huge silver Venetian mirrors, gilded pilasters, and a six-foot flower bouquet, the rooms have fine classic furnishings and everything for the up-to-date office: oversized desk, ergonomic chair, speaker phones, direct Internet access, dedicated fax and phone lines, copiers, printers, and your own coffee maker. The result is elegant and professional.

The white marble bathrooms have an abundance of lush towels and the all-cotton sheets on the custom-designed beds are of the highest quality. You can even choose from a dozen pillow options: from the five-foot body pillow to the buckwheat model. Now there's a first.

On the second floor there's a comfortable lounge over-looking Lexington Avenue and a series of rooms for business meetings. Plus, the hotel's Woodstock Spa offers the latest in exercise equipment and a full menu of body treatments. The Benjamin conveys the manners and the confidence of a hotel that has been there forever. Very soon, the Waldorf might be the hotel to go to when the Benjamin is fully booked.

GUEST SERVICES: Business center; fitness center and spa; Internet access; kitchen facilities; minibar; restaurant/bar; room service; safe in room; TV/VCR; valet parking.

NEIGHBORHOOD RESTAURANTS: Terrance Brennan's Seafood and Chop House, 565 Lexington Ave. at 50th St., 715-2400 (surf-and-turf from one of New York's best chefs); Smith and Wollensky, 797 Third Ave. at 49th St., 753-1530 (one of New York's top steakhouses; huge portions; great wine list); Chin Chin, 216 E. 49th St. bet. 2nd and 3rd Aves., 888-4555 (one of the city's best and most original Chinese restaurants; delicious, creative fare).

The Bentley Hotel

500 East 62nd Street bet. York Avenue and FDR Drive
Phone: (212) 644-6000 Fax: (212) 759-5023
Number of Rooms: 197
Price Range: Standard, $255–$285; deluxe, $325–$375;
suite, $425–$700
Credit Cards: All major
www.nychotels.com

JUST WEST OF THE EAST RIVER and north of Sutton Place and the 59th Street Bridge is a new deluxe boutique hotel, the Bentley. What a soothing oasis this is! Enter the lobby, with its 18-foot soaring ceiling, and a Zen-like ambiance surrounds you: All is cool and tranquil. The floor-to-ceiling white curtains swish gently while the recessed lights create a restful yet theatrical glow. Modern furnishings and muted colors add to the feeling of peace. Even the little hideaway of a library beckons you to stop, sip a cappuccino, and read the daily paper.

Try to book a room on the south or west side of the building—the sweeping, unobstructed views of the Queensboro Bridge, the East River, and the Roosevelt Island Tram are spectacular. (When was the last time you woke up to the sight of boats going by your window?) The room furnishings, too, aim to soothe the senses and the soul. Bathrooms, marbled and mirrored with all the little extras, could be photographed for *Architectural Digest*. Other amenities include a continental breakfast with Krispy Kreme doughnuts.

One block from the restaurants, singles bars, and movie theaters of First Avenue and a 20–30 minute walk from Midtown, the Bentley is closer to the city shuffle than its riverside address suggests, yet it is miles away in terms of peace and quiet. It's perfect for the busy traveler in search of an urban sanctuary. Relax. You're in good hands.

GUEST SERVICES: Complimentary breakfast; CD player; restaurant/bar; fitness center (affiliated); TV/VCR; valet parking; room service (limited).

NEIGHBORHOOD RESTAURANTS: Merchants NY, 1125 1st Ave. at 62nd St., 832-1551 (hip bar/restaurant serving standard American fare); Maya, 1191 1st Ave. bet. 64th and 65th Sts., 585-1818 (creative Mexican fare in a fun atmosphere); John's Pizza, 408 E. 64th St. bet. 1st and York Aves., 935-2895 (outstanding pizza in casual surroundings; great for kids).

Bevy's Soho Loft

70 Mercer Street bet. Broome and Spring Streets
Phone: (212) 431-8214 Fax: (212) 343-0218
Number of Rooms: 3
Price Range: Two large bedrooms with shared bath $180 and
$200; luxury double with private bath, $280; annex apartment
on nearby Prince Street $900 for 3-night minimum.
Credit Cards: None
www.sohobevy.com

TUCKED INTO THE REMOTE REACHES of lower Soho
is an old industrial loft building that houses one of New
York's unique hospitality experiences. Bevy's Loft is a wonderfully warm, inviting, somewhat funky, bohemian salon
that is Soho's only bed and breakfast. Run by Bevy, a friendly and free-spirited lady, the Loft consists of a living room
with a fireplace, a dining area with a giant table, two bathrooms, and three large bedrooms, all with high ceilings.
Furniture and decorations are an eclectic mix of flea market
finds and gifts from many of the artist guests, resulting in an
effect that is both cool and quirky. The general feeling here
is one of an extended family with Bevy doting over her
many children—more of a family home than a traditional
B&B. Neighbors drop in for a friendly chat or to tell a funny
story. Guests hang out in the living room sipping coffee.
Former guests swing by to say hello and drop off a gift. This
is clearly an important stop on many a far-flung traveler's
itinerary. Feeling thirsty? The fridge is yours. Hungry? Help
yourself. It's more like home than home.

There is a graciousness to the Soho dimensions of the
rooms that is soothing and relaxing. Each of the three bedrooms is different with its own closet solutions, bedspreads,
and décor, but they are similar in style. The giant loft windows look out over Mercer Street and a back courtyard.
There is a good sweet feeling here. It's in the tone of the
voices, the comfort of the beds. Everyone is so nice.
Everything is so welcoming. The Soho location is also a

big, big plus. You're right in the center of where it's happening. Bevy's Loft is as much a feeling and an atmosphere as it is a place. You take it with you once you leave, and you want to come back for more. The problem is you may never want to leave.

GUEST SERVICES: Complimentary breakfast; kitchen facilities; TV.

NEIGHBORHOOD RESTAURANTS: Balthazar, 80 Spring St. bet. Broadway and Crosby, 965-1414 (a re-creation of a Paris bistro; one of the city's hottest restaurants); Jerry's, 101 Prince St. bet. Greene and Mercer Sts., 966-9464 (American fare in a dinerlike setting); Broome Street Bar, 363 West Broadway at Broome St., 925-2086 (a Soho classic for burgers, salads, and beers).

Broadway Bed & Breakfast Inn

264 West 46th Street bet. Broadway and Eighth Avenue
Phone: (212) 997-9200 Fax: (212) 768-2897
Number of Rooms: 41
Price Range: Single, $89–$110; double, $129–$189;
luxury suites, $199
Credit Cards: All major
www.broadwayinn.com

ALTHOUGH THE NAME "Bed & Breakfast Inn" may conjure up images of country houses with four-poster beds and roaring fireplaces, don't be fooled. No Ye Olde B&B here. Remember where you are now: This is Times Square. This is the Theater District. This is the heart of New York City. The Broadway Bed & Breakfast Inn offers inexpensive, clean, and relatively attractive, if somewhat simple, accommodations. The lobby does make a gesture in the "inn" direction.

It's small and welcoming, with two cozy couches and numerous tables where guests hang out sipping the complimentary coffee and relaxing after a hard day of touristing. The Tchaikovsky on the sound system adds a refined touch. The exposed brick wall features photographs of old New York and the overall atmosphere is social, convivial, and friendly. A restful interlude in a restive city.

The small bedrooms offer little in terms of luxuries. Remember, you're here for price and location. Furniture is basic and functional, but the emphasis on cleanliness is reassuring, especially in an area of the city famous for its dirt and grime. Broadway posters serve to decorate. Fortunately, too, the noise level is low: a second layer of windows having been recently installed.

The Broadway Bed & Breakfast Inn is a good choice for budget-conscious theatergoers who plan to see a number of shows and want to stay nearby, or for those who want to be in the heart of New York City and want a simple, clean room in a safe, welcoming place. Given its plans, over time this may develop into the kind of theater district boutique hotel that would make it a laid-back alternative to its slicker Schrager-owned neighbors. In the meantime, you could be pleasantly surprised.

GUEST SERVICES: Business center; car service; complimentary continental breakfast; Internet access; restaurant; discounted parking; refrigerators; TV.

NEIGHBORHOOD RESTAURANTS: Becco, 355 W. 46th St. bet. 8th and 9th Aves., 397-7597 (charming country Italian with good food at good prices); Plataforma, 316 W. 49th St. bet. 8th and 9th Aves., 245-0505 (authentic *riodizio* restaurant); View, 1535 Broadway at 45th St., 704-8900 (revolving restaurant/bar, spectacular views); Zen Palate, 663 9th Ave. at 46th St., 582-1669 (nouvelle Asian vegetarian, soothing atmosphere).

Bryant Park Hotel

40 West 40th Street bet. Fifth and Sixth Avenues
Phone: (212) 869-0100 Fax: (212) 869-4446
Number of Rooms: 130, 7 suites
Price Range: $325–$875
Credit Cards: All major
www.thebryantpark.com
Email: Sdeangelis@phgmc.com (Sales Dept.)

ON VALENTINE'S DAY, 2001, this instantly famous, petite, black art deco skyscraper unveiled itself as one of New York's most luxurious and romantic boutique hotels. Across the street from the New York Public Library and the adjacent Bryant Park, this Midtown hostelry has been designed as a retreat for the international fashion and entertainment crowd. A Zen-like simplicity, harmony, and tranquility pervades the rooms, which are furnished in ultra-contemporary style. Be sure to book a table at Ilo, the hotel's hot 3-star restaurant, or descend to the moody candlelit Cellar bar where the young, beautiful, and oh-so-stylish patrons are served expensive cocktails by the young, beautiful, and oh-so-stylish staff. Wasn't that Bryan Ferry and Jade Jagger over there in the corner?

GUEST SERVICES: Room service; full spa; gym; restaurant (Ilo); Internet access; private dining; cellar bar and lounge. NEIGHBORHOOD RESTAURANTS: DB Bistro Moderne, 55 W. 44th St. between 5th and 6th Aves., 391-2400 (vibrant, upscale bistro fare by top chef Daniel Boulud); Branzini, 299 Madison Ave. at 41st St., 557-3340 (Mediterranean fare in a pretty space that's part of the Library Hotel); Crestanello, 475 Fifth Ave. bet 40th and 41st Sts., 545-9996 (spacious Italian caffe known for its pastries, gelato, and salads).

Carlton Hotel

22 East 29th Street bet. Fifth and Madison Avenues
Phone: (212) 532-4100 Fax: (212) 889-8683
Number of Rooms: 320
Price Range: $195–$315
Credit Cards: All major
www.carltonhotel-ny.com

TUCKED INTO A CORNER of Murray Hill, in a 100-year-old building with an ornate facade festooned with iron balustrades and intricate stone carvings, stands one of the best unheralded hotels in town. Newly renovated, the Carlton is the hostelry of choice for young international travelers in the know and families who want to know.

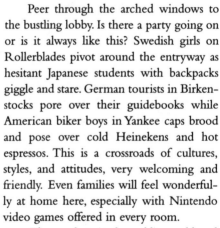

Peer through the arched windows to the bustling lobby. Is there a party going on or is it always like this? Swedish girls on Rollerblades pivot around the entryway as hesitant Japanese students with backpacks giggle and stare. German tourists in Birkenstocks pore over their guidebooks while American biker boys in Yankee caps brood and pose over cold Heinekens and hot espressos. This is a crossroads of cultures, styles, and attitudes, very welcoming and friendly. Even families will feel wonderfully at home here, especially with Nintendo video games offered in every room.

The modest-sized, sparkling gold and mirrored lobby features a comfortable lounge with bar and coffee service. Upstairs, the halls are clean and bright, with tasteful sconces adorning the walls. Many of the rooms are particularly large, newly renovated, and some even have views of the Empire State Building. So when making a reservation, be sure to request one of these. The contemporary American furnishings are new and serviceable, and the bathrooms have been re-done in ceramic tile with beige marble countertops. Noise levels are low and the rooms are blissfully quiet.

The Carlton offers a clean, well-lighted place, and an accommodating staff at an affordable price. At the Carlton, everyone seems to be having a good time, even the people who work there. They must be doing something right.

GUEST SERVICES: Business center; complimentary continental breakfast; health spa; health club; Internet access; room service; minibar; restaurant/bar; room service; safe in room; TV/VCR; 24-hour concierge; valet parking.

NEIGHBORHOOD RESTAURANTS: I Trulli, 122 E. 27th St. bet. Park and Lexington Aves., 481-7372 (enchanting southern Italian); Les Halles, 411 Park Avenue South at 29th St., 679-4111 (delicious meat-oriented French bistro); Café Journal, 47 E. 29th St. bet. Park and Madison Aves., 447-1823 (French café best for simple breakfast/lunch).

Hotel Casablanca

147 West 43rd Street bet. Sixth Ave. and Broadway
Phone: (212) 869-1212 Fax: (212) 391-7585
Toll free: (888)-922-7225
Number of Rooms: 48
Price Range: $265–$375
Credit Cards: All major except DC
www.casablancahotel.com

"I CAME TO CASABLANCA FOR THE WATERS." Rick, as we all know by now, was misinformed about the nonexistent waters of Casablanca, but this intimate luxury boutique hotel off Times Square is truly an oasis. Developed and owned by Henry Kallan, whose previous efforts include the Hotel Wales and the Hotel Elysée, this 48-room townhouse evokes a miniature Moroccan fantasy world. When you are standing in the small but beautifully realized oak-paneled lobby, your eye is immediately drawn to the mural of sun-drenched Moroccan rooftops dominating the formal staircase. Ascend to the second-floor lounge called (what else) Rick's Café, and help yourself to the complimentary cappuccino and Pepperidge Farm cookies. In the evening, the caffeine and sweets give way to wine and cheese. The café's

North African theme is reflected in the Moroccan-style shutters and a color scheme of warm browns with dashes of greens, reds, and blues. Custom-made leather and rattan chairs and blue-and-white Moorish mosaic tiles complete the picture. Walls are book-lined, featuring an eclectic collection of easy-reading titles ranging from *Hollywood Babylon* to the Ingrid Bergman biography *You Must Remember This.*

Upstairs (there are six floors) the rooms and halls carry on the North African theme both in colors and the custom-made furnishings. Corridors are highlighted by Italian Murano glass fixtures, and the walls are festooned with antique Berber scarves. Room amenities include fresh flowers, comfy terrycloth bathrobes, and complimentary soft drinks, bottled water, and sweets. Clearly the intent here is to evoke a sense of exotic locales and distant lands of another time, but the reality is up-to-the-minute, cutting-edge services amid comfort and luxury. What's a ceiling fan without nearby Internet access? And Oriental rugs are mere anachronisms unless the planned cybercafe is in operation. Also on the drawing board are big-screen TV movies with popcorn and candlelight. Captain Renault and Major Stroesser never had it this good.

The Casablanca is the epitome of the well-appointed boutique hotel, examples of which are sprouting up around the city. High-concept, high-quality furnishings, and great attention to details matter in a space that resembles a European inn more than a large, impersonal city hotel. And if it really is the exotic that you seek, just outside the door and around the corner is Times Square, with all the exotica any time-worn traveler could possibly desire.

GUEST SERVICES: Complimentary breakfast; TV/VCR; complimentary wine/hors d'oeuvres weekdays; complimentary movie rentals; complimentary access to New York Sports Club.

NEIGHBORHOOD RESTAURANT: Bryant Park Grill, 25 W. 40th bet. 5th and 6th Aves., 840-6500 (lively dining pavilion with good American fare).

Chambers Hotel

15 West 56th St. bet. Fifth and Sixth Avenues
Phone: (212) 974-5656 Fax: (212) 974-5657
Number of Rooms: 77
Price Range: $295–$1,600
Credit Cards: All major
www.chambersnyc.com

DOWNTOWN IN STYLE AND SENSIBILITY, uptown in luxury and location, the Chambers, which opened in March 2001, is a discreet, deluxe boutique hotel that oozes cool and sophistication, but with a sense of humor. Muted house music greets you as you pass through the massive wooden doors. There's no name outside, but you're just steps away from Trump Tower and around the corner from Tiffany's and Bergdorf's. With neighbors like these who needs a sign? Prada-clad, model-thin receptionists greet you in hushed foreign inflections. Contemporary art graces the walls of every floor and public space. This place is smart and very knowing. Rooms are large-ish and decorated in soft colors and luxurious materials. A perfect spot for the well-heeled international sophisticate who wants to be uptown, but has downtown in his heart.

GUEST SERVICES: Data port; Internet access; flat-screen TVs; room service; gym; restaurant (Town).
NEIGHBORHOOD RESTAURANTS: Bay Leaf, 49 W. 56th St. between 5th and 6th Aves., 957-1818 (light Indian fare with Western touches); Topaz Thai, 127 W. 56th St. between 6th and 7th Aves., 957-8020; Rue 57, 60 W. 57th St. at 6th Ave., 307-5656 (always crowded American-French brasserie).

Chelsea Hotel

222 West 23rd Street bet. Seventh and Eighth Avenues
Phone: (212) 243-3700 Fax: (212) 243-3700
Number of Rooms: 400 (300 long-term)
Price Range: Single, $125–$175; double, $150–$250;
suite, $300 & up
Credit Cards: All major
www.hotelchelsea.com

THIS IS A SENTIMENTAL CHOICE—one that has more to do with history and reputation than comfort and security. And like many of life's more interesting (and satisfying) experiences, it should be tried at least once, if only so that you can say you did.

Visiting the Chelsea, with its striking balconied exterior, is more akin to visiting a shrine or a memorial than a resting spot for the weary traveler. This is our Père La Chaise without the gravestones, our Poet's Corner without the plaques. Those who have been guests or have lived here over the years form a roll call of some of the twentieth century's greatest names in the arts. When the names of Mark Twain and Sid Vicious, Sarah Bernhardt and Jimi Hendrix, Dylan Thomas and Madonna, Arthur Miller and Patti Smith can be paired off in the same sentence, and their likes can be found sleeping under the same roof, it is evident that homage must be paid. Yes, this is where Sid Vicious killed his inamorata Nancy Spungen. Yes, this is where Dylan Thomas died after drinking twenty-plus whiskeys at the White Horse Tavern. Yes, this is where Thomas Wolfe wrote *You Can't Go Home Again,* and where Virgil Thompson lived for many years. Okay. We've paid homage. But when the veil of myth and memory drops away, you are left with a rather unseemly and threadbare Victorian pile quite in need of an update. Nonetheless, a funky charm does pervade the lobby area, adorned with the manager's private art collection, consisting primarily of his friends' works. Those comprising the eclectic mix of young people around the front desk look as if they had been lifted from a '90s version of Edward Hopper's *Nighthawks*. And the plaster-of-Paris women on a swing suspended from the ceiling add a David Lynch touch.

Upstairs, there are more friends' paintings lining the linoleum-floored hallways. Words like "dark" and "gloomy," may at first leap to mind, but rooms are big and decorated with unique Salvation Army accents. The only evident room service appears to be an offer from the local members of the world's oldest profession, whose unofficial alfresco headquarters is rumored to be several blocks westward. Consider it local color.

But go to the Chelsea. Go to see it if not to stay there. Movies have been made there, books have been written about it, and all those famous people must have been drawn there for some reason. Perhaps you'll be drawn in, too.

GUEST SERVICES: Kitchen facilities in some rooms; TV with cable. NEIGHBORHOOD RESTAURANTS: Chelsea Bistro & Bar, 358 W. 23rd St. bet. 8th and 9th Aves., 727-2026 (pretty store-front bistro with good French food); East of Eighth, 254 W. 23rd St. bet. 7th and 8th Aves., 352-0705 (warm and inviting café with ambitious menu); Krispy Kreme, 265 W. 23rd St. bet. 7th and 8th Aves., 620-0111 (arguably the best doughnuts in New York).

Designed by Hubert de Pirran 1884

Chelsea Inn

46 West 17th Street bet. Fifth and Sixth Avenues
Phone: (212) 645-8989 Fax: (212) 645-1903
Number of Rooms: 25
Price Range: Single, $99; quad, $209
Credit Cards: All major
www.chelseainn.com

IT'S INEXPENSIVE, SAFE, and in a convenient location. Created out of the lower floors of two combined nineteenth-century townhouses, the Chelsea Inn offers generous space and good value in somewhat understated surroundings. Targeted to the budget and student travel market, the place has the feel of an old country home decorated with your grandmother's cast-off furniture and mismatched items picked up at the 26th Street flea market. The rooms are generously large and the suites are huge; all have kitchenettes, a happy extra if you're on a tight budget. Lower-priced rooms share baths and amenities are few.

The fact that the developers, owners, and managers of the Chelsea Inn are all the same people is a big plus, and the woman behind the front desk is friendly and willing to do whatever she can to make your stay enjoyable. The inn's location in the Flatiron district, one of the city's hottest neighborhoods at the moment, makes it ideal if you want to be in the heart of Silicon Alley or near Midtown, the Village, the photo district, the Toy Center and Gift Building. The real estate adage that the three most important considerations for any property are location, location, location aptly describe the appeal of the Chelsea Inn. Oh, and let's not forget price, too.

GUEST SERVICES: Kitchen facilities; safe in room; TV.
NEIGHBORHOOD RESTAURANTS: Da Umberto, 107 West 17th St. bet. 6th and 7th Aves., 989-0303 (excellent Italian food in a lively setting); AZ, 21 W. 17th St. bet. 5th and 6th Aves., 691-8888 (cool restaurant for downtown hipsters with French/American menu).

Chelsea Savoy

204 West 23rd Street bet. Seventh and Eighth Avenues
Phone: (212) 929-9353 Fax: (212) 741-6309
Number of Rooms: 90
Price Range: Single, $99–$115; standard, $125–$165;
quad, $145–$195
Credit Cards: All major
www.chelseasavoynyc.com

THE CHOICE OF APPEALING hotel accommodations in Chelsea is rather limited, which is a shame given the vibrancy of the neighborhood and its proximity to the Flatiron district, Silicon Alley, and many of the city's trendier locales. Into this void enters the Chelsea Savoy, a recently opened boutique hotel that caters to the same kind of people who live and work in the area: hip, smart, image-conscious, and not willing to pay a lot of money for a hotel room. To this end, the Chelsea Savoy succeeds on all counts. The deco furnishings and large C-shaped sitting area in the glass façade lobby, along with the too-cool, attractive staff members, belie the fact that upstairs it's a no-frills operation all the way. Singles are . . . well, singles. So leave your friends at home as the postage-stamp-sized spaces leave little extra

room for paperbacks and paramours. Furnishings tend to follow the standard midlevel hotel style, with floral bedspreads taking a bow on the hotel stage. Baths are clean with lots of pink marble, and the towels are new, thick, and fluffy.

Nonetheless, the Chelsea Savoy is a good deal in a vital neighborhood and has little competition from its neighbors. It's affordable, it's spotlessly clean, it's new, and it has ambitions to hip boutique hotel status. It may not have gotten there yet, but neither have the prices. It's a fine downtown choice and getting better all the time.

GUEST SERVICES: Internet access; restaurant/bar; room service; safe in room; TV.
NEIGHBORHOOD RESTAURANTS: Negril Island Spice, 362 W. 23rd St. bet. 8th and 9th Aves., 807-6411 (handsome Jamaican restaurant with good cheap fare); Caffè Buon Gusto Due, 249 W. 26th St. bet. 7th and 8th Aves., 929-1345 (good brick-oven pizza).

City Club

55 West 44th Street bet. Fifth and Sixth Avenues
Phone: (212) 921-5500 Fax: (212) 944-5544
Email: reservation@cityclubhotel.com
Number of Rooms: 65, including a grand duplex,
bilevel suites, and junior suites.
Price Range: $225–$1,200
www.cityclubhotel.com

THE CITY CLUB OPENED IN JANUARY 2002 and is an intimate, "painfully chic" luxury boutique hotel that offers style with a dash of elegance and lots of personalized service. "Think a hip Lowell or a Midtown Mercer," said owner/developer Jeffrey Klein, a well-known maven of the Park Avenue benefit-party circuit. Located on a block filled with New York "institutions," the hotel is nestled between the legendary Algonquin (one of the city's great literary landmarks) and the Iroquois, across the street from the Royalton, and just down from the Harvard Club and New York Yacht Club. Classy company, indeed, and stiff competition. City Club is also adjacent to DB Bistro Moderne, one of New York's hottest and most highly acclaimed new restaurants.

GUEST SERVICES: Complimentary pass to New York Sports Club; high-speed Internet access; DVD; CD library; valet service.

NEIGHBORHOOD RESTAURANTS: 44, 44 W. 44th St. bet. 5th and 6th Aves., 944-9416 (delicious, innovative fare in very modern surroundings); Chikubu, 12 East 44th St. bet. 5th and Madison Aves. 818-0715 (excellent authentic Japanese with loyal following).

Country Inn the City

270 West 77th Street
Phone: (212) 580-4183
Number of Rooms: 4 (two people maximum per room)
Price Range: $150–$210; three-night minimum stay
Credit Cards: None
House Rules: No smoking, no children under 12, and no pets
www.countryinnthecity.com

IMAGINE WHAT IT WOULD BE LIKE to have a good friend in the city who has a beautiful, turn-of-the-century townhouse in a quiet residential neighborhood where you could stay in your own spacious room with a sumptuous, comfortable bed any time you wanted. You could come and

go as you pleased. You could even cook if you felt like it (but who would want to with all the great restaurants just a few steps away). The place would be clean, quiet, and elegantly decorated, and you'd practically have it all to yourself. You'd be living like a rich New Yorker, without having to take care of the place or pay the real estate taxes. Well, who needs friends when you have Country Inn the City, a four-room B&B on the Upper West Side that is one of New York's secret little gems.

The rooms are large and gracious, and they were recently renovated so that each has a kitchenette, bathroom, and bedroom with sitting area, yet the old-world charm of the original moldings, details, and fireplaces has been maintained. Furnishings throughout the inn strike a well-balanced mixture of antiques and reproductions. Nice touches extend to the maroon carpeted stairway lined with vases, antique clocks, and chairs. The huge elk's head at the top of the staircase adds a whimsical, idiosyncratic flair to the otherwise elegant appointments.

If you're lucky enough to be here during warm weather, try to book the room on the top floor, where you can sip a glass of wine on your private terrace perched over the neighboring brownstones. Its leafy trellis and potted plants, along with a table and chairs, provide your own little Eden amid the urban din.

Country Inn the City is a dreamlike place. Staying here gives you the sense of being a real New Yorker, living in a real neighborhood in a really nice apartment. But unlike most New Yorkers, you are coddled amid serenity and graciousness. A rare combination resulting in a most satisfying stay.

GUEST SERVICES: Complimentary breakfast; kitchen facilities; safe in room; TV.

NEIGHBORHOOD RESTAURANTS: Big Nick's Burger Joint, 2175 Broadway at 76th St., 362-9238 (good, cheap burgers; local favorite); Zabars, 2245 Broadway at 80th St., 787-2003 (New York institution; gourmet deli); Isabella's, 359 Columbus Ave. at 77th St., 724-2100 (neighborhood hangout with decent Italian fare).

Crowne Plaza at the United Nations

304 East 42nd Street bet. First and Second Avenues
Phone: (212) 986-8800 Fax: (212) 986-1758
Number of Rooms: 300
Price Range: Standard, $239–$379; executive, $269–$409
Credit Cards: All major
www.crowneplaza-un.com

WAY, WAY EAST ON 42ND STREET—far from the 42nd Street of Port Authority, Times Square, Disney, and Grand Central—there is a quieter, gentler 42nd Street. Here, not far from the United Nations and the Ford Foundation and just north of Tudor City, is the charming, European-style Crowne Plaza at the United Nations.

Formerly the Tudor Hotel, this distinctive landmarked property was recently purchased by the Crowne Plaza chain, and, and, thankfully, all of its character has been left intact. It still feels very much like the independent boutique hotel that was here for over seventy-five years, its recent major renovation notwithstanding. This end of East 42nd Street is a part of town that is nice and peaceful. The hotel's narrow lobby bustles with activity (mostly U.N. types, business travelers, and European tourists); while its black-and-white stone floors, square columns, and muted lighting create the feeling of a junior baronial reception hall (the influence of nearby Tudor

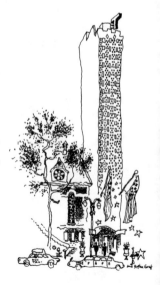

City perhaps?). The young staff is perky and solicitous. Rooms are on the small side with newish, functional dark wood furniture. Beautiful old leaded-glass windows are distinctive and many overlook the courtyards and towers of Tudor City and parts of the Manhattan skyline. (Try to get a corner room if possible.) Closets are ample and clean and contain an iron and a safe. Italian-marble bathrooms come equipped with all the amenities, including a hair dryer and a phone. (This is New York, remember.)

What is wonderful about this hotel is that it feels like a find; it's been here just east of the heart of Midtown for all these years, yet somehow it has managed to stay undiscovered. A delightful hotel with an upbeat personality that serves as an appropriate counterbalance to its more infamous neighbors farther west.

GUEST SERVICES: Coffee maker; fitness center; minibar; restaurant/bar; trouser press; TV.

NEIGHBORHOOD RESTAURANTS: Palm, 837 2nd Ave. bet. 44th and 45th Sts., 687-2953 (New York institution for lobsters and steaks); Phoenix Garden, 242 E. 40th St. at 2nd Ave., 983-6666 (classic Cantonese cooking); Ambassador Grill, 1 UN Plaza at 44th St. and 1st Ave., 702-5014 (handsome setting and good American fare).

1871 House

130 East 62nd Street bet. Park and Lexington Avenues
Phone: (212) 756-8823 Fax: (212) 588-0995
Number of Rooms: 10 Rooms
Price Range: $139–$385
Credit Cards: All major
www.1871house.com
info@1871house.com

IMAGINE—NEW ENGLAND COUNTRY CHARM
just steps from Park Avenue! This delightfully warm and welcoming bed and breakfast is located in a classic five-story
brownstone on one of New York's loveliest, tree-lined blocks.
Proprietor Lia Raum and her husband, Warren, have furnished this wonderfully special place with treasures gleaned
from Connecticut antiques stores and flea markets. The result
is a feeling of home and hearth, as you would dream it to be.
More country inn than urban B&B, here personal attention,
good taste, and loving care are evident in every detail. Hand-
stitched quilts, hooked rugs, sleigh beds, and sporting prints
and paintings abound. Most bedrooms feature original moldings and working fireplaces. Windows look out on either the
leafy, quiet street or the tree-shaded back garden. If you can,
book the romantic Cottage room, with its sun-drenched
second-floor terrace. This book was written expressly to
unearth gems like 1871 House—a lovely "country" hideaway
in one of New York's most elegant neighborhoods.

GUEST SERVICES: Internet access; TV.
NEIGHBORHOOD RESTAURANTS: Jojo, 160 E. 64th St.
between Lexington and Third Aves., 223-5656 (opulent surroundings showcase the top-notch fare of Jean-Georges
Vongerichten); Madame Romaine de Lyons, 132 E. 61st St.
between Park and Lexington Aves., 759-5200 (cozy breakfast joint famous for its variety of omelettes and fantastic
baked goods).

Hotel Elysée

60 East 54th Street bet. Madison and Park Avenues
Phone: (800) 535-9733 or (212) 753-1066
Fax: (212) 980-9278
Number of Rooms: 89 rooms, 12 suites
Price Range: Standard, $295–$365; piano suite, $995
Credit Cards: All major
www.elyseehotel.com
members@aol.com/elysee99/

VLADIMIR HOROWITZ PLAYED HERE; Tennessee Williams died here; Tallulah Bankhead drank here; and other Hollywood, Broadway, and literary legends too numerous to mention made the Hotel Elysée their home in New York at one time or another over the past sixty-odd years. (We do have it on good account that George Washington did not sleep here.)

The ghosts of its illustrious past lend a welcome, somewhat notorious cachet to this elegant boutique hotel in Midtown. But the Elysée is not a hotel to rest on its history no matter how illustrious or infamous it might be. A recent multimillion-dollar renovation has transformed the hotel into a sophisticated European-style country-inn-in-the-city, one whose seemingly effortless attention to detail leaves the most discerning guest impressed, relaxed, and feeling pampered. Everything is done with taste and understated elegance. The small marble lobby is formal yet welcoming, and the friendly professional staff greet you by name and with warm, friendly smiles. Trompe l'oeil ivy festoons the wall along the lobby staircase that leads to a delightfully

45

cheery second-floor guest lounge. Here you can relax over tea and cookies or wine and cheese, or you can ensconce yourself in an overstuffed armchair with a leather-bound Victorian novel from the adjacent library.

Try to book one of the rooms with an enclosed greenhouse terrace and delight in the view over that great modernist monument, Mies van der Rohe's Seagram Building. Most rooms are of moderate size and decorated in muted, conservative color schemes; they are well appointed with antique furnishings and fine linens and bed covers. Bathrooms feature gray marble and brass fixtures and offer all the amenities of a first-class hotel.

Just off the downstairs lobby, the legendary Monkey Bar harks back to the hotel's dramatic roots. Although the black-tied swells of the 1930s gossip pages can no longer be found drinking their bone-dry martinis and vintage champagne, the energy level is high and the air is filled with smoke and possibility. The adjacent restaurant of the same name evokes the ocean-liner dining rooms of yesteryear, with its plush banquettes, deco décor, dramatic lighting, and black-and-white photos of famous former patrons. And the food is as first class as the surroundings.

The Elysée—elegant, intimate, stylishly sophisticated, affordable, and right in the middle of Manhattan. If only Tallulah and Tennessee could see it now. . . .

GUEST SERVICES: Complimentary continental breakfast; Internet access; minibar; restaurant/bar; room service; tea, wine, and hors d'oeuvres; TV/VCR.

NEIGHBORHOOD RESTAURANTS: Aquavit, 13 W. 54th St. between 5th and 6th Aves., 307-7311 (fabulously creative Scandinavian fare in dramatic setting); Bice, 7 E. 54th St. between 5th and Madison Aves., 688-1999 (slick, chic, pricey Italian); PJ Clarke's, 915 3rd Ave. at 55th St., 317-1616 (quintessential New York bar for burgers, beer, and atmosphere).

Empire Hotel

44 West 63rd Street at Broadway
Phone: (212) 265-7400 Fax: (212) 315-0349
Number of Rooms: 350
Price Range: Single, $200; double, $225; suite, $300;
two-bedroom suite, $650
Credit Cards: All major
www.empirehotel.com

SOMETIMES ONLY THE CLOSEST WILL DO. The Empire's proximity to Lincoln Center and its location at the gateway to the Upper West Side make it worthy of mention. This is definitely *the* place to stay if you are in town for the numerous opera, dance, classical music, or theatrical performances held across the street. Or if you want a good, solid, full-service corporate hotel that is a little bit away from the frenzy of Midtown but close enough for a quick cab ride or a ten- to fifteen-minute stroll. That Central Park is only a block away is also a big plus, especially for runners, walkers, and weekenders.

The uniformed staff is exceptionally polite and upbeat. The double-height lobby is buffed and polished with cream-colored marble, Oriental carpets, and gleaming Italianate wooden furnishings—corporate law firm as New York hostelry. We're talking about serious, efficient, no-nonsense hotel-running here. No whirring Casablanca ceiling fans, Philippe Starck headboards, or tattooed movie stars at the Empire. Here it's business, thank you very much. Pleasantly so, however, and the result is very relaxing and comfortable. It's reassuring to know that you are in the hands of people who know what they are doing and go to great lengths to take care of you. The medium-sized rooms are rather simply done with contemporary furnishings, but all the requisite amenities are provided.

With 350 rooms, the Empire still has the feel of a small hotel and is certainly one of the few hotels on the Upper West Side worth recommending. And after a seemingly six-hour evening of Wagner, that is often just what you need.

GUEST SERVICES: Bar on premises; CD library; CD/cassette player; hair dryers in every room; laundry services; minibar; restaurant; room service; TV with VCR.
NEIGHBORHOOD RESTAURANTS: Gabriel, 11 W. 60th St. bet. Broadway and Columbus Aves., 956-4600 (good Italian food, many celebrities); Picholine, 35 W. 64th St. bet. CPW and Broadway, 724-8585 (great Mediterranean fare from master chef Terrance Brennan).

Fitzpatrick Manhattan Hotel

687 Lexington Avenue bet. 56th and 57th Streets
Phone: (212) 355-0100 Fax: (212) 308-5166
Number of Rooms: 92 (40 rooms, 52 one-bedroom suites)
Price Range: Executive room, $190; suite, $280
Credit Cards: All major
www.fitzpatrickhotels.com

Fitzpatrick Grand Central Hotel

141 East 44th Street bet. Lexington and Third Avenues
Phone: (212) 351-6800 Fax: (212) 818-1747
Number of Rooms: 155
Price Range: Deluxe single, $199; deluxe double, $399
single suite, $525; double suite, $525; garden suites, $500
Liam Neeson Penthouse, $1,000
Credit Cards: All major
www.fitzpatrickhotels.com

Fitzpatrick Manhattan Hotel

DUBLIN. CORK. BUNRATTY. Names that evoke the words of Yeats and Joyce, the dramas of O'Casey and Wilde, a thousand different shades of green, and the creamy head on a pint of Guinness. They are also the cities where the Fitzpatrick family has hotels in addition to these on the east side of town. And those names only hint at what you will find inside these Irish charmers. What weary traveler wouldn't be uplifted by the sound of an Irish-lilted welcome and a smile from a green-jacketed colleen right out of Dublin central casting. The front-desk clock is set at local Irish time, and that laughing red-haired group sipping Bushmills in the bar off the green-carpeted lobby appears about to burst into "Danny Boy."

Irish ambiance and friendliness mix with corporate amenities and efficiency to create a home-away-from-home atmosphere. The ample rooms offer comfortable, contemporary furnishings and watercolors of the homeland, as well as fax machines, modem connections, and trouser presses.

For the homesick and hungry, Fitzers Restaurant and Bar, off the main lobby, serves a traditional Irish breakfast as well as other Irish specialties such as lamb stew, oak-smoked salmon, and chicken Hibernia in a whiskey sauce. One of the city's best pours of Guinness can be had from the convivial bartender, who counts such notable ex-pats as Liam Neeson, Stephen Rea, and Sinead O'Connor among his patrons, as well as the occasional Kennedy or two. So if you're Irish or part Irish or just happen to like Ireland, you will feel very much at home at the Fitzpatrick.

Fitzpatrick Grand Central

LIKE ITS SISTER HOTEL, the Fitzpatrick Grand Central is a delightfully friendly hotel that is long on infectious Irish charm and hospitality. While at the Fitzpatrick Manhattan accommodations are mostly suites, here there are large rooms with canopied beds; the amenities are similar. Bathrooms are luxurious with blue marble walls, and throughout the hotel, there is an atmosphere of goodwill and cheer. Everyone seems to be having a great time. Even the décor echoes this: it is bright with cheery colors and comfortable nooks and crannies, where you can relax. And don't miss Wheeltappers Pub, behind the lobby, which doubles as a genuine mini-museum of the Irish National Railroad. It's about as close to Dublin as you are likely to get on this side of the Atlantic.

GUEST SERVICES (MANHATTAN HOTEL): Parking; restaurant/ bar; room service; TV.

NEIGHBORHOOD RESTAURANTS: (MANHATTAN HOTEL): Le Colonial, 149 E. 57th St. bet. Lexington and 3rd Aves., 752-0808 (chic spot with delicious Southeast Asian fare); Shun Lee Palace, 155 E. 55th St. bet. Lexington and 3rd Aves., 371-8844 (elegant Chinese with top Shanghai fare); Prime Grill, 60 East 49th St. bet. Park and Madison Aves., 692-9292 (something for everyone, including steaks and sushi).

GUEST SERVICES: (GRAND CENTRAL HOTEL): Fitness center off premises; Internet access; restaurant/bar; room service; safe in room; TV; valet parking.

NEIGHBORHOOD RESTAURANTS: (GRAND CENTRAL HOTEL): Chikubu, 12 E. 44th St. bet. 5th and Madison Aves., 818-0715 (top Japanese restaurant featuring the cuisine of Kyoto; popular with business crowd); Luna Blu, 246 E. 44th St. bet. 2nd and 3rd Aves., 681-6541 Italian with good regional fare).

The Franklin Hotel

164 East 87th Street bet. Lexington and Third Avenues
Phone: (212) 369-1000 Fax: (212) 369-1000
Number of Rooms: 53
Price Range: Single, $169; double, $189
Credit Cards: All major
www.franklinhotel.com

WHAT WAS IT ABOUT THE FRANKLIN HOTEL that put me in a movie mode? Why was I thinking of J. J. Gittes in *Chinatown* and Jean-Louis Trintignant at the opening of *The Conformist*? Maybe it was the classic red neon sign over the entrance. Or was it the darkly elegant marble lobby? Or the dramatically lit hallways? Well, whatever your cinematic bent, if you are looking for high New York style at low non–New York prices, there is no better place to stay than the Franklin.

A cross between an updated version of where Philip Marlowe might have stayed in a Raymond Chandler story and a hip hostelry for fashion-conscious trendsetters, the Franklin offers minimal modernist décor, art deco furnishings, and many personal touches. The Franklin does a lot with limited space. While there are two tiny public rooms off the lobby, there is Mozart on the sound system, free frothy cappuccino, all the daily newspapers, and original artwork on

the walls (including a genuine Picasso print from the owner's collection). It all reflects a knowing New York style that addresses the needs and tastes of the most cosmopolitan of guests. And at the Franklin all this New York elegance and sophistication doesn't come with any New York attitude or indifference. The staff here exudes a spirit of friendliness and helpfulness that is more Midwest than Manhatttan.

While rooms may be small and have limited closet and drawer space, they are dramatically designed with gauzy white bed canopies, kidney-curved desks, and custom-built steel furniture. An obsession with cleanliness is evident throughout, and each bathroom has a hair dryer and a basket of Neutrogena products. Guests can request free CDs and videos from the hotel's own extensive catalog.

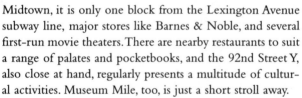

Although the Franklin is a ten- to fifteen-minute cab ride from Midtown, it is only one block from the Lexington Avenue subway line, major stores like Barnes & Noble, and several first-run movie theaters. There are nearby restaurants to suit a range of palates and pocketbooks, and the 92nd Street Y, also close at hand, regularly presents a multitude of cultural activities. Museum Mile, too, is just a short stroll away.

While you may not encounter Barbara Stanwyck or Veronica Lake on your first visit, you will be heartily welcomed at this all-but-private clublike hotel. And at such reasonable prices, you're unlikely to stay anywhere else again.

GUEST SERVICES: Complimentary breakfast; CD library; CD player; complimentary breakfast buffet; hair dryer in every room; parking; TV with cable and VCR.

NEIGHBORHOOD RESTAURANTS: Carino, 1710 2nd Ave. bet. 88th and 89th Sts., 860-0566 (cozy neighborhood trattoria; great food, low prices); Elaine's, 1703 2nd Ave. bet. 88th and 89th Sts., 534-8103 (famous celebrity hangout); Lexington Avenue Coffee Shop, 1226 Lexington Ave. at 83rd St., 288-0057 (classic 1950s diner; great coffee and simple food).

Gershwin Hotel

7 East 27th Street bet. Fifth and Madison Avenues
Phone: (212) 545-8000 Fax: (212) 684-5546
Number of Rooms: 150
Price Range: Dormitory bed, $29.99;
standard room, $169–$209; superior room, $189–$245;
suites, $250 and up
Credit Cards: All major
www.gershwinhotel.com
reservations@gershwinhotel.com

WHEN YOU PULL UP TO THE GERSHWIN HOTEL'S red-painted façade, those huge sculpted light fixtures that greet you are meant to give the illusion that the hotel is on fire. And that sums up what a visit to the Gershwin is all about: zaniness, craziness, a sense of hipness and humor. Recently renovated, it is also clean and has comfortable, albeit modest accommodations at very reasonable prices.

Enter the lobby that is part Pee-Wee Herman's Fun House and part Roy Lichtenstein homage. It feels like you're in the middle of an independent film festival for fringe artists and auteurs dressed in nose rings, tattoos, combat boots, and grunge clothing. The gothic Red Room bar off the lobby is dark and candlelit and looks set-up for an Electric Kool-Aid Acid Test. The adjacent Back Room offers nightly light entertainment and is clearly a meeting ground for young hipsters.

This is a hotel with an entire floor reserved only for models, who according to the manager, require "special handling." Each floor is dedicated to a different artist, whose work decorates the halls. Rooms are plain and simple, decorated with stylized, budget-conscious furnishings. Bathrooms are pleasantly spacious and clean. For those just needing a bed to flop on for the night, there are shared dormitory facilities with bunk beds.

The Gershwin is a slick hangout for models, rock stars, and the young, trendy, international set. It's perfect if you're looking for where the action is and a shared hip-hop communal camaraderie. Comfort and service are not really the issue here. But no one seems to care. Oh, to be twenty and staying at the Gershwin. Imagine the possibilities.

GUEST SERVICES: Cafe/Bar; Internet access; laundry service; parking; safe in room; TV.

NEIGHBORHOOD RESTAURANTS: Tabla, 11 Madison Ave. at 25th St., 889-0667 (excellent upscale Indian); The Gamut Bistro Lounge, 102 E. 25th St. bet. Park Avenue South and Lexington Aves., 598-4555 (bistro lounge serving great steak sandwiches).

The Giraffe

365 Park Avenue South (at 26th Street)
Phone: (212) 685-7700 Fax: (212) 685 7711
Number of Rooms: 73 rooms; 12 suites
Price Range: $295–$425
Credit Cards: All major
www.hotelgiraffe.com

THE GIRAFFE EXUDES A PARISIAN FLAIR combining modern design with contemporary American sensibility. Opened in April 2000, this upscale boutique hotel features many nice touches: comfortable club chairs, French doors, Juliet balconies, and I-Love-New-York views. Rooms are comfortable, sophisticated, and stylish with lots of indulgent amenities like quilted satin bedcovers and thick terry robes. Is this what a crossing on the *Normandie* was like? Be sure to try the wonderful Mediterranean fare at Sciuscia, the hotel's new restaurant.

GUEST SERVICES: Continental breakfast; cordless telephones; Internet access; room service.
NEIGHBORHOOD RESTAURANTS: Dos Caminos, 373 Park Ave. between 26th and 27th Sts., 294-1000 (gorgeous, sexy, fun, vibrant Mexican); Park Bistro, 414 Park Ave. South at 28th St., 689-1360 (updated French in bistro setting); Picasso Café, 43 E. 29th St., 696-4488 (terrific pizzas in a casual setting).

The Gorham Hotel

136 West 55th Street bet. Sixth and Seventh Avenues
Phone: (212) 245-1800 Fax: (212) 582-8332
Number of Rooms: 115
Price Range: Single, $215–$400; double, $225–$440; suite,
$255–$460; penthouse suite, $525
Credit Cards: All major
www.gorhamhotel.com
reservations@gorhamhotel.com

"CATHERINE DENEUVE STAYED HERE way back when," trumpeted one of the Gorham's staff members.

Opened in 1929, the newly renovated Gorham offers a comfortable European feel in a stylish setting. With a refreshing lack of attitude, the emphasis here is on friendly, personalized service, good-sized rooms, and affordable prices, all in a convenient location. An independent Italian-owned enterprise, the hotel enjoys a loyal clientele, endeared by its idiosyncratic character.

The massive chandelier at the entrance looks straight out of *The Phantom of the Opera* and the gilded lobby with its black leather couches and Persian rugs convey a certain discreet bourgeois charm. Upstairs, there are fresh flowers in the brightly lit hallways. Rooms are comfortably spacious and done in a contemporary Euro-style with red lacquer furnishings. While the bedspread pattern may induce vertigo in some, bathrooms are pleasing with cool marble, a large tub, and all the requisite gadgets and toiletries. Every room has a kitchenette equipped with microwave and refrigerator/freezer. Perfect for weekend family trips, the Gorham provides for cribs and rollaway beds in the rooms and will arrange babysitting services.

The Gorham has the great advantage of being centrally located. It is directly across from City Center and only two blocks from Carnegie Hall and the Museum of Modern Art. From here, you could walk anywhere in Midtown, to the Theater District, or up to Central Park (just think of the money you could save on taxi fares). While the Gorham may offer charms not entirely unique to New York, its prime location, emphasis on service, renovated, comfortable rooms, and reasonable prices make it an excellent choice for business travelers and families.

GUEST SERVICES: Breakfast buffet; fax/computer facilities; fitness center; Internet access; kitchen facilities; refrigerator/freezer; parking; room service; TV; VCR on request.
NEIGHBORHOOD RESTAURANTS: Bricco, 304 W. 56th St. bet. 8th and 9th Aves., 245-7160 (casual Italian with very good food); East, 251 W. 55th St. bet. Broadway and 8th Ave., 581-2240 (decent Japanese at reasonable prices); Carnegie Deli, 854 7th Ave. at 55th St., 757-2245 (great New York deli).

Gracie Inn

502 East 81st Street bet. York and East End Avenues
Phone: (212) 628-1700 Fax: (212) 628-6420
Number of Rooms: 12 suites
Price Range: Studio suite, $199;
two-bedroom penthouse suite, $449
Credit Cards: All major
www.gracieinn.com

THE GRACIE INN, tucked away on an unremarkable side street on the Upper East Side of Manhattan, is distinguished first by the fact that it exists here at all, this being a residential neighborhood consisting almost exclusively of townhouses and apartment buildings.

The inn is a charming, quirky, homey B&B that was converted some time ago from a boardinghouse. Each of the twelve rooms has a kitchenette and a private bath, and the rooms are decorated with an eccentric and eclectic collection of odds and ends. Faux antique furniture, pastel southwestern color schemes, artificial flowers, stenciled floors, and department store landscapes predominate—with the best of intentions. Rooms are smallish, but cozy and exceptionally clean, the best being those on the upper floors with views and terraces. There is no public space to speak of except for the tiny area around the front desk, filled with brochures from local eateries and nearby shops. Something about the place brings *Fawlty Towers* to mind, so that you almost expect John Cleese to emerge from the back office.

The location, only blocks from Gracie Mansion, the official residence of the city's mayor, ensures security and quiet in what is already a peaceful and calm area. The Metropolitan Museum of Art is just a ten- to fifteen-minute walk away. And the lack of affordable, cozy accommodations in the neighborhood makes it ideal if you are visiting friends nearby or museum hopping.

GUEST SERVICES: Complimentary breakfast; Internet access; kitchen facilities; room service; TV.

NEIGHBORHOOD RESTAURANTS: Cafe Trevi, 1570 1st Ave. bet. 81st and 82nd Sts., 249-0040 (delicious Northern Italian in relaxed setting); Primavera, 1578 1st Ave. at 82nd St., 861-8608 (one of the best old-fashioned Italian restaurants in the city); Ottomanelli's, 1626 York Ave. bet. 85th and 86th Sts., 772-7722 (great for burgers, pastas, pizzas, and salads).

Gramercy Park Hotel

2 Lexington Avenue at 21st Street
Phone: (212) 475-4320 Fax: (212) 505-0535
Number of Rooms: 360 rooms; 150 suites
Price Range: $155–$230
Credit Cards: All major
www.gramercyparkhotel.com

"BUT HE'S/SHE'S GOT A GREAT PERSONALITY."
We've all either heard or used that line before. And the
Gramercy Park Hotel has personality to spare. There is something about its shabby-chic, old-world charm that is both
cool and sexy. There is a sense of possibility in the air, a feeling that anything can happen here.

Purported to be the hotel of choice among rock stars,
models, and artists, the hotel is located on what is probably
one of the loveliest blocks in town, overlooking beautiful
and graceful Gramercy Park. (Hotel guests are provided with
a key to the park, one of New York's most exclusive privi-
leges.) Back inside, things start to get more interesting.

The lobby, with its dusty crystal chandeliers, scattered
potted plants, and mismatched worn chairs, looks as if it has
leapt full-blown off the pages of a Dashiell Hammett story.
And the cast of characters bustling through the lobby at all
hours reminds one of *Grand Hotel*. Isn't that Baron Von
Geigern over there in the armchair? You get the idea: fallen
aristocrats, fading ballerinas, would-be celebrities, and lots and
lots of Europeans. This is New York at its melting-pot best.

Upstairs, rooms are spacious. Many are the size of a one-
bedroom apartment in New York, and offer plenty of closet
space. Bathrooms, too, are large, with their old fixtures
adding to the aging character of the place. Some of the
rooms include such nice touches as original moldings and
decorative marble fireplaces, and afford lovely views of the
park and the surrounding prewar buildings.

Great location, low prices, and the cinematic downtown atmosphere are all reasons to stay at the Gramercy

Park Hotel. While not luxurious, it is a true New York experience. And like a fine single malt whiskey, fresh oysters on the half shell, or Proust, once tried, you may become a true believer forever.

GUEST SERVICES: Beauty/barber salon; parking nearby; restaurant/bar; room service; safe in room; TV.

NEIGHBORHOOD RESTAURANTS: Bolo, 23 E. 22nd St. bet. Broadway and Park Ave. South, 228-2200 (excellent and imaginative Spanish-influenced fare); Pete's Tavern, 129 E. 18th St. at Irving Pl., 473-7676 (classic old New York tavern for basic Italian/American fare); Angelo & Maxie's, 233 Park Ave. South at 19th St., 220-9200 (great steak at reasonable prices).

Habitat

130 East 57th Street bet. Park and Lexington Avenues
Phone: (212) 753-8841 Fax: (212) 838-4767
Number of rooms: 350
Price Range: $79 (shared bath)–$365 (penthouse suites)
Credit Cards: All major
www.habitatny.com

LOCATION, LOCATION, LOCATION . . . WITH STYLE and at a very reasonable price—this is what Habitat is all about. Built in 1926 as the Allerton House, a hotel for single women, this art deco-y property has been recently renovated into an efficient, cool, and comfortable destination for the young, budget-conscious traveler. Just two blocks from Bloomingdale's and a few minutes' walk to the high end shopping districts of Fifth and Madison Avenues, Habitat is for those who want to be in the center of it all but don't want to pay the prices of the traditional Midtown hotel. Here you'll ascend by stairs or elevator to a second-floor lobby with soft moody lighting, long serpentine designer-couch, and wafting Calder-like mobile overhead. This is a budget hotel disguised as a hip hostelry for the international set. Sure, many of the rooms are spare and simple and share a bath, but hey, this is New York. You never know whom you are going to meet on the way to the shower. It's not only fun but it's one of the city's great bargains.

If your finances allow, book one of their penthouse studios, and don't miss their Opia restaurant off the main lobby. It's very now, very elegant, and very popular and has gotten great reviews. Save your money on the room and spend it at the restaurant on the person you met brushing your teeth.

NEIGHBORHOOD RESTAURANTS: Teodora, 141 E. 57th St. between Lexington and 3rd Aves., 826-7101 (quaint, unpretentious Northern Italian); Benihana of Tokyo, 120 E. 56th St. between Lexington and Park Aves., 593-1627 (Japanese spot known for the knife-wielding masters at the teppanyaki grills).

Hotel Dylan

52 East 41st Street bet. Park and Madison Avenues
Phone: (212) 338-0500 Fax: (212) 338-0569
Number of Rooms: 107 rooms; 2 suites
Price Range: $295–$445
Credit Cards: All major
www.hoteldylan.com
Dylanhotelres@aol.com

LOCATED IN A CLASSIC 1903 BEAUX-ARTS building that once housed the Chemists Club, this graceful boutique hotel is just around the corner from Grand Central Terminal. Opened in October 2000, the old-meets-new transformation of this landmark structure has resulted in an evocative, timeless atmosphere where contemporary chic melds with turn-of-the-century detailing. The majestic curved staircase, the Gothic-inspired Alchemy Suite, the carved plaster ornamentation and stained-glass windows have been retained as symbols of Old New York at its grandest. Due to its origins as a private club, Dylan's rooms are larger than those found in many other boutique hotels—most have entrance foyers and 11-foot ceilings. Room design is luxurious—with Carrara marble bathrooms—soothing, and contemporary.

GUEST SERVICES: Business services; fitness center; Internet access; room service; voicemail.

NEIGHBORHOOD RESTAURANTS: Salmon River, 3 E. 40th St. between 5th and Madison Aves., 481-7887 (contemporary room with a winning seafood menu); Bryant Park Grill, 25 W. 40th St. between 5th and 6th Aves., 840-6500 (large terraced American spot popular with after-work singles); Branzini, 299 Madison Avenue at 41st St., 557-3340 (Mediterranean fare in a pretty space that's part of the Library Hotel).

Hotel 41 at Times Square

206 West 41st Street bet. Seventh and Eighth Avenues
Phone: (212) 703-8600 Fax: (212) 302-0895
Number of Rooms: 47
Price Range: $129–$489
www.hotel41.com
www.boutiquehg.com

THE FACT THAT HOTEL 41 IS LOCATED next door to the Nederlander Theater, home of the musical *Rent*, just about says it all. This is Broadway, baby. Nestled amid the vibrancy, bounce, and hustle of Times Square and the Theater District, this intimate haven conforms perfectly to the formula for the successful boutique hotel: appealing décor and superior service rounded out by competitive rates, a distinctive personality, and a singular location. Opened on July 11, 2002, Hotel 41 is located in a classic 100-year-old building that has been completely renovated and transformed into this modern, sophisticated hostelry.

A glass of complimentary Chardonnay greets you upon arrival—believe me, you'll need it after negotiating your way here. Remember, this is the "Crossroads of the World." The lobby is small and a little cramped, but there are enough sophisticated touches and friendly and helpful staffers to keep your focus elsewhere. "Can I have a refill, maybe?" Upstairs the guest rooms are comfortable with straightforward, yet plush and stylish furnishings. Rooms are on the small side, but are blissfully quiet due to the double-paned windows. The spacious all-white bathrooms feature all the extra niceties one could want. Who doesn't love a terry-cloth bathrobe, fluffy towels, and Aveda bath products? If its extra room you want, book a junior suite or, better yet, the penthouse suite with its own furnished private terrace and wet bar. Although there are literally hundreds of restaurants within walking distance, don't miss the hotel's own Oasis Lounge—a high-energy bar and restaurant just off the lobby that is perfect for pre- and-post theater eating and drinking.

Hotel 41 works on a number of different levels. It's hip enough to appeal to the young and the chic; its location appeals to the tourist, the theatergoer, and those wanting to be near Midtown, and the moderate prices can be enjoyed by everyone. What else could you want in a boutique hotel?

GUEST SERVICES: Valet parking; 24-hour room service; high-speed Internet access.

NEIGHBORHOOD RESTAURANTS: Chez Josephine, 414 W. 42nd St. bet. 9th and 10th Aves., 594-1925 (lively, whimsical spot that's one of the best in the theater district); Easy Internet Café, 234 W. 42nd St. bet. 7th and 8th Aves., 398-0775 (world's largest Internet café serving casual café fare); Yoshinoya, 255 W. 42nd St bet. 7th and 8th Aves., 703-9940 (good, inexpensive Japanese fast food).

The Hudson

356 West 58th Street bet. Eighth and Ninth Avenues
Phone: (212) 554-6000 Fax: (212) 554-6001
Number of rooms: 1,000; 2 suites
Price Range: $145–$500
Credit Cards: All major
www.Hudsonhotel.com
Hudson@Ianschrager.com

FUN, SEXY, AND PULSING with the vibrant energy of frenetic, fashionable New Yorkers, the Hudson is brought to you by the supercharged team of cutting-edge designer Philippe Starck and master hotelier Ian Schrager. This 1,000-room, innovatively audacious homage to hipness was conceived as a privileged environment for the beau monde. It's big, clever, entertaining, and operatic, with a seemingly nonstop party happening at the Hudson Bar on the second floor. Stop by and watch black-clad, unshaven men and stiletto-heeled women sip chilled Cosmopolitans, flirt, and groove to hip-hop. This is the land of velvet ropes, guest lists, and jangling cell phones where you need to be "in" to "get in."

GUEST SERVICES: Room service; full cable access; gift shop; valet parking; spa; gym; restaurant.
NEIGHBORHOOD RESTAURANTS: Bricco, 304 W. 56th St. bet. 8th and 9th Aves., 245-7160 (casual trattoria with tasty Italian standards); Eatery, 798 Ninth Ave. at 53rd St., 765-7080 (sleek spot with modern comfort food); Jean-Georges, 1 Central Park West at 60th St., 299-3900 (innovative fare by master chef Jean-Georges Vongerichten).

Incentra Village House

32 Eighth Avenue bet. West 12th and Jane Streets
Phone: (212) 206-0007 Fax: (212) 604-0625
Number of Rooms: 12
Price Range: Single, $119; suite, $199
Credit Cards: All major

THE FARTHER WEST YOU GO in Greenwich Village, the easier it is to get lost. With numbered streets giving way to names and seeming to run at odd angles, and with the absence of tall buildings, it's somewhat difficult to get oriented.

In the heart of this maze lies the Incentra Village House, a charming and inexpensive little guest house. Occupying two 1841 redbrick townhouses, the Incentra is friendly and welcoming, and the young people who run it are especially kind and helpful. The double parlor serving as the lobby is as charming as lobbies come: two fireplaces, a baby grand piano, book-lined shelves, gilded antique mirrors, and beautiful, huge windows with giant drapes. Guests are given both a room key and a key to the front door, so they can come and go as they please. It's like having your own apartment in the Village.

Finding your room is a journey in itself as you wander down narrow corridors and up winding old stairways. Most of the twelve rooms have kitchens and working fireplaces. With no coherent floor plan, some of the rooms have lots of angles, levels, and steps; each is individually decorated and named, resulting in a charming hodgepodge. The Maine Room, with its four-poster double bed and matching bureau from a farmhouse in Maine, is a particular favorite. Be sure to request one of the back rooms that overlook a classic little garden and the nearby townhouses. The front rooms face Eighth Avenue and can be noisy.

Although the house is looked after with care by people who love it, there is a feeling of the slightly old and a certain mustiness. The result is that the overall atmosphere is one of a deluxe youth hostel. Nonetheless, if you are on a somewhat restricted budget or are a student traveler, the Incentra is a great choice. Its location at the confluence of several of the city's most vibrant communities, and its proximity to some of downtown's coolest restaurants, bars, and stores, allows access to so much life within a few minutes' walk. There are but a few delightful places to stay in the Village, and this being one of them makes it a very special place indeed.

GUEST SERVICES: Working fireplaces; kitchen facilities; TV.
NEIGHBORHOOD RESTAURANTS: Rio Mar, 7 9th Ave. at Little W. 12th St., 243-9015 (dark and mysterious Spanish restaurant with good, reasonably priced food); Tortilla Flats, 767 Washington St. at W. 12th St., 243-1053 (funky, fun Tex-Mex joint); La Ripaille, 605 Hudson St. bet. W. 12th and Bethune Sts., 255-4406 (cozy, romantic, country French bistro).

The Inn at Irving Place

56 Irving Place bet. 17th and 18th Streets
Phone: (212) 533-4600 Fax: (212) 533-4611
Number of Rooms: 12
Price Range: $295–$495
Credit Cards: All major
www.innatirving.com

IT'S DIFFICULT TO IMAGINE what Anton Dvorák and
Evelyn Nesbit had in common. One wrote the *New World
Symphony*. The other, known as the Girl in the Red Velvet
Swing, became infamous as the inamorata of Stanford White,
who was shot dead nearby at the old Madison Square
Garden by Ms. Nesbit's jealous husband, Harry Thaw. At the
Inn at Irving Place, two of the twelve rooms have been
named after these turn-of-the-century New York luminar-
ies, as well as a number of other denizens of this historic
neighborhood, including Sarah Bernhardt, Washington
Irving, and even Mr. White himself. Although
there is no obvious connection between the
names and the rooms (I couldn't find the red
velvet swing), each room is spacious and decorated with an emphasis on antique luxury.

probably the most
charming hotel in the world.

The Elsie de Wolfe
Room (she lived across
the street) features a
bamboo bed and an art
nouveau loveseat. The
Ellen Olenska Room
(the temptress in Edith
Wharton's *The Age of
Innocence*) is decorated in
Americanized Empire
style and has a window
seat with a view of
Irving Place, Gramercy

Park, and the Chrysler Building. The O. Henry Room, overlooking the courtyard garden, has an iron-framed double bed covered with a silk damask duvet and four fluffy pillows, and a fireplace graced by a fan-shaped brass screen and a triptych mirror over the mantle.

Created from a pair of 1830s townhouses, this lovely boutique inn is reminiscent of a cozy Victorian home where charm, comfort, care, and a wisp of romance are the order of the day. The décor is full of Oriental rugs, period antiques, original moldings, daily fresh flowers, and attention to detail. And when was the last time you enveloped yourself in a Frette robe after a hot bath? Or poured yourself a good strong double in a leaded crystal glass from an honor-system liquor cart? Or dealt with a staff who look as if they've stepped out of a Ralph Lauren ad? And they're friendly and funny and helpful, too. Let them convince you to enjoy the five-course afternoon tea that is served in the Lady Mendl tea salon in the north parlor.

The Inn at Irving Place is very special. There are few places like it in the city. So turn back the clock a hundred years, summon the resident ghosts of yesteryear, and immerse yourself in an age of elegance. P.S. Don't look for an awning or sign upon arrival. They like to keep this treasure carefully hidden.

GUEST SERVICES: Complimentary breakfast; Internet access; fitness center nearby; minibar; parking nearby; safe in room; room service; tea salon, dessert parlor, and martini lounge on premises; TV.

NEIGHBORHOOD RESTAURANTS: Friend of a Farmer, 77 Irving Place bet. 18th and 19th Sts., 477-2188 (country food in cottage setting); Verbena, 54 Irving Pl. bet. 17th and 18th Sts., 260-5454 (elegant spot serving creative American fare); Yama, 122 E. 17th St. at Irving Pl., 475-0969 (great sushi); Irving on Irving, 52 Irving Pl. at 17th St., 358-1300 (bistro fare).

Inn New York City

266 West 71st Street
Phone: (212) 580-1900 Fax: (212) 580-4437
Number of Rooms: 4 suites
Price Range: Deluxe suite, $375–$575
Credit Cards: Amex, MC, Visa
www.innnewyorkcity.com

THE FACT THAT THERE IS NO SIGN OUT FRONT should be a giveaway. The proprietors want anonymity. In fact, Ruth Mensch, an interior designer, and her daughter, Elyn, a fabric designer, are trying hard to keep this wonderful little secret to themselves and their steady stream of loyal customers. Unfortunately for them and fortunately for the rest of us, word is getting out. This romantic Victorian inn, situated in a beautiful turn-of-the-century brownstone, graces one of the Upper West Side's loveliest residential tree-lined streets.

Inside you'll find four lavishly furnished suites, each with its own distinctive style and personality. The one-bedroom

duplex Vermont Suite, with its private entrance, exudes English country charm; and its Victorian iron staircase spirals down to a delightfully secluded bedroom. The grand first-floor Opera Suite is over 50-feet long and has a private terrace reached through French doors. Twelve-foot ceilings, stained-glass panels, ornate moldings, and a working fireplace highlight the luxuriously elegant space. There's even a baby grand piano for your ivory-tickling pleasure. Hedonists might elect to stay in the Spa Suite, an entire floor devoted to sybaritic pleasure. A built-in king-sized bed sits on a raised platform surrounded by antique chestnut armoires, a mirrored mantel, and period wooden shutters. The oversized private spa offers a double-sized Jacuzzi, sauna, bidet, and glass-block-enclosed shower. Perfect for a romantic interlude or just a relaxed weekend getaway. The top-floor Library Suite is graced by fourteen-foot wood-beamed ceilings and magnificent leaded-glass skylights. Spacious and comfortable, the living room features a fireplace, exposed-brick walls, and an entire wall of books. No wonder one of the conductors at the Metropolitan Opera stays here when in town.

The attention to pleasure and comfort in even the smallest details is what is most delightful at this unique haven. Forget any preconceived notions of a continental breakfast. Here you'll find bagels, carrot cake, muffins, fruit, muesli, wonderful coffee, orange and grapefruit juices, Camembert and cream cheese, and quiche. There are even pancakes for the true trencherman. Shoes a bit scuffed? Every room has an electric shoe polisher. Worn out after a long day? Sink into a hot tub with its own headrest, then wrap yourself afterward in one of the deluxe terry-cloth robes and pour a glass of imported Chardonnay from the bottle cooling in the fridge. With fresh long-stemmed roses in the vase and Ella Fitzgerald scatting on the CD player, it doesn't get much better than this.

No surprise, then, that some of their most devoted guests come from right around the neighborhood—stressed New Yorkers who yearn for a brief escape into a rarefied fin de siècle world of romance and luxury, charm and comfort. You can get there from here. Just don't tell anybody how or where.

GUEST SERVICES: Complimentary breakfast and wine; CD player; Internet access; kitchen facilities; laundry service; safe in room; TV.
NEIGHBORHOOD RESTAURANTS: Café La Fortuna, 69 W. 71st St. at Columbus Ave., 724-5846 (classic old-fashioned Italian café); Café Luxembourg, 200 W. 70th St. bet. Amsterdam and West End Aves., 873-7411 (sophisticated, art deco French bistro); Café des Artistes, 1 W. 67th St. bet. Central Park West and Columbus Ave.

Inn on 23rd Street

131 West 23rd Street bet. Sixth and Seventh Avenues
Phone: (212) 463-0330 Fax: (212) 463-0302
Number of rooms: 11; 4 mini-suites, 1 large suite
Price Range: $199–$259; suite, $350
Credit Cards: All major except the Discover card
www.innon23rd.com; innon23rd@aol.com

THIS ECLECTIC CHARMER in the heart of Chelsea is one of New York's best bed and breakfasts. Opened in May 1999 in a restored five-story classic 19th-century townhouse, it's a great find for anyone who wants beautiful, spacious accommodations combined with personalized charm within walking distance of Midtown, SoHo, the Village, and Gramercy Park. Each of the 11 rooms has its own theme and features the proprietor's tasteful mix of antiques, family heirlooms, and contemporary art. Their names tempt you for what lies within: the Victorian Room, the Quilt Room, the Rosewood Room, the 40s Room, and Ken's Cabin, to name a few. Give the friendly owners, Annette and Barry Fisherman, a call, and make your way to one of the city's great undiscovered hostelries.

GUEST SERVICES: Breakfast service by the New York Culinary Institute; private baths; two-line telephone with data port; voicemail.
NEIGHBORHOOD RESTAURANTS: Arezzo, 46 W. 22nd St. between 5th and 6th Aves., 206-0555 (modern space with pricey Tuscan fare); Basil, 206 W. 23rd St. between 7th and 8th Aves., 242-1014 (traditional Thai with interesting choices); Half King, 505 W. 23rd St. at 10th Ave., 462-4300 (Irish pub fare in a sunny room).

Iroquois New York

49 West 44th Street bet. Fifth and Sixth Avenues
Phone: (212) 840-3080 Fax: (212) 398-1754
Number of Rooms: 105; 9 suites
Price Range: Room, $225; suite, $525
Credit Cards: All major
www.iroquoisny.com

THE IROQUOIS NEW YORK is the quintessential boutique hotel. One of only three hotels in Gotham to be selected as a member of the Small Luxury Hotels of the World, the Iroquois combines a dignified elegance with a stylish smartness and has become quietly popular with the fashion and celebrity set.

The newest addition to this deluxe, full-service hotel is the two-star restaurant Triomphe, recently voted best new Theater District restaurant by *New York* magazine.

Pass under the glass-and-bronze marquee and through the double-hung mahogany French doors, and you enter a small, beautifully designed lobby. Relax in the adjacent Library, lined with leather-bound volumes of the classics. Order a scotch and sink into one of the overstuffed armchairs in the James Dean Lounge, a quiet, cozy wood-paneled cocktail bar. Barber's "Adagio for Strings" playing on the sound system completes the picture.

Each guest suite is elegantly designed around a different subject: from Broadway to Fashion, Art, and Photography. (Suite 803 is the James Dean Suite with photographs and memorabilia of the actor who lived here in his pre-*Rebel Without a Cause* days.) "Restful green" is the color of choice for the guest rooms and each is decorated with French residential furnishings and includes all the comforts of home: cable TV, CD/radio, minibar, bottled water, bathroom slippers, terry-cloth robes, and more. The floor-to-ceiling marble bathrooms are so welcoming and lavish, you just want to order in room service and dry your hair all day.

Located directly across the street from the Royalton, just to the right of the Algonquin, and down the block from the Harvard and New York Yacht clubs, the Iroquois is in the center of where it is happening in Midtown. Times Square and the Theater District, Grand Central Station, Rockefeller Center, and Fifth Avenue's shopping strip are all within a few minutes' walk. This lovely gem of a boutique hotel is relatively undiscovered, but it won't be for long.

GUEST SERVICES: CD player; fitness center; Internet access; minibar; restaurant/bar; room service; safe in room.
NEIGHBORHOOD RESTAURANTS: 44 Royalton, 44 West 44th St. bet. 5th and 6th Aves., 944-9416 (chic and stylish hotel restaurant with creative menu; popular with fashion/publishing crowd); Trattoria Dopo Teatro, 125 West 44th St. bet. Broadway and 6th Ave., 869-2849 (charming, casual Italian).

Jolly Hotel
Madison Towers

22 East 38th Street (at Madison Avenue)
Phone: (212) 802-0600 or (800) 221-2626
Fax: (212) 447-0747
Number of Rooms: 252
Price Range: Single, $250; double, $460
Credit Cards: All major
www.jollyhotels.it, www.jollymadison.com

WHY IS IT that we love everything Italian? Who hasn't fallen in
love at one time or another with the
food, the wine, the countryside, the
music, the architecture, the fashion,
the sleek automobiles, and the beautiful people of that lovely country?
Italian charm and style can be very
seductive but often come at a cost
that only the Armani-clad, the
Gucci-shod, the Bulgari-draped, and
the Portofino-bound can afford. But
here at the Jolly Hotel Madison Towers in Murray Hill, owned
by Jolly Hotels, the largest hotel chain in Italy, the prices bear
little relation to the lovely Italianate furnishings, warm surroundings, and friendly service that await you. The cost is but
a small step or two above a budget hotel, yet the far superior
accommodations are those of a moderate-class hotel.

Come in off the quiet side street, and meander through
the spacious lobby and on up to the mezzanine. Italian paintings and crystal sconces adorn the walls. Beautiful lamps, fresh
flowers, gilded mirrors, and marble and wrought iron tables
accentuate the welcoming space. This looks and feels really
nice. Am I going to be let down once I get to my room? Not
a chance. Upstairs, everything is new, clean, and comfortable,

each room, although on the small side, having been fully renovated in 1994. The dark wood and brass furniture is tasteful, and the desk and sitting area are pleasantly roomy. The decorative paintings are rather pretty, and a number of the rooms look out on the Empire State Building.

Tense after a long day? At the third-floor Oriental Spa, steam or sauna your cares away, or have your back walked on by a masseuse in a darkened shiatsu room. You'll never feel this relaxed again—worth the price of a room on its own. A little culture? The little jewel that is the Morgan Library is just a ninety-second walk down the street. Reasonable rates, convenient location, and all the necessary comforts served up with that little extra Italian something that makes all the difference. *Arrivederci Roma. Buongiorno* Jolly Madison.

GUEST SERVICES: Business center; health club; Internet access; minibar; restaurant/bar; room service; safe on premises; TV; valet parking.

NEIGHBORHOOD RESTAURANTS: Asia de Cuba, 237 Madison Ave. bet. 37th and 38th Sts. (in Morgans Hotel; a hip scene with good Asian-Cuban fare); Les Halles, 411 Park Ave. South, bet. 28th and 29th Sts., 679-4111 (worth the walk for excellent French bistro fare; beef a specialty); Dock's Oyster Bar, 633 3rd Ave. at 40th St., 986-8080; Icon (in the W hotel), 130 East 39th St. at Lexington Ave., 592-8888.

The Kimberly

145 East 50th Street bet. Third and Lexington Avenues
Phone: (212) 755-0400 Fax: (212) 486-6915
Number of Rooms: 186
Price Range: Deluxe room, $219–$325; one-bedroom suite,
$265–$780; two-bedroom suite, $409–$675
Credit Cards: All major
www.kimberlyhotel.com

TUCKED HALF A BLOCK BEHIND THE WALDORF–ASTORIA lies one of New York's secret and charming treasures: the first-class Kimberly hotel. Catering largely to a well-heeled South American and European clientele, The Kimberly goes about its business in an understated, self-assured manner and seems quite happy to operate this way.

The Kimberly's apartmentlike accommodations, most of which include fully equipped kitchens, are perfect for stays of several weeks or more and for those with business in Midtown. Rooms are spacious, furnished in a classic continental style, embellished with floral patterns, and many have outdoor balconies. Step outside and, even with the Midtown noise, you can imagine yourself right in the middle of a Woody Allen picture. Then take a cruise up the Hudson on the hotel's 75-foot yacht—New York doesn't get more cinematic than this.

Because the New York Health and Racquet Club and the Kimberly share an owner, guests have complimentary use of the club's facilities, which include swimming pools, tennis, squash, and racquetball courts as well as workout equipment. For the more sybaritic, spa treatments are also available.

The Kimberly is one of New York's best-kept secrets.

GUEST SERVICES: Fax machine; fitness center; kitchen; TV with cable; yacht.

NEIGHBORHOOD RESTAURANTS: Olica, 145 East 50th St. bet. Lexington and Third Aves., 583-0001 (Bistro with refined French fare); Lutèce 249 East 50th St. bet. 2nd and 3rd Aves., 752-2225 (haute French at haute prices); One51, 151 East 50th St. bet. Lexington and Third Aves., 753-1144 (offers dinner only and dancing from 10 P.M. to 4 A.M.); Montparnasse, 230 East 51st St. bet. 2nd and 3rd Aves., 758-6633 (French brasserie with tasty contemporary fare).

The Kitano New York

66 Park Avenue (at 38th Street)
Phone: (212) 885-7000 Fax: (212) 885-7100
Number of Rooms: 149; 18 suites
Price Range: Single, $245; Tatami suite, $1995
Credit Cards: All major
www.kitano.com

THE FIRST THING YOU HEAR IS SILENCE, maybe a whisper or a murmur, nothing more. Your eyes notice the exquisite details and tasteful furnishings of the warm mahogany and marble lobby. Then you see it: the big black dog with his tongue sticking out. Don't worry, he won't bite. Fernando Botero's bronze dog sculpture serves as a silent sentinel watching over the hushed comings and goings at one of the city's most elegant small luxury hotels.

Everything about the Kitano is meditative, spiritual, and reverent of its Eastern origins. The $50-million renovation in 1995 has respected the hotel's history both as the first Japanese-owned hotel in New York, and a property that was owned by the Rockefeller family in the late nineteenth century. That gives you a sense of what the Kitano is all about—a hotel fit for a billionaire that respects the culture of its Far Eastern owners. East meets West here in an exquisite harmony of Western-style luxury and comfort with Asian sensuality and tradition. Along with the sleek hotel piano bar on the mezzanine, there is a private tearoom with a Zen-like calm for quieter, more contemplative libations. The sun-dappled Garden Cafe, which caters to the more Occidental palate, is complemented by the premier restaurant, Nadaman Hakubai, where amidst a sedate understated setting, Japanese chefs prepare elegant *kaiseki* dishes.

All the 149 ample-sized guest rooms are appointed with handsome custom-made furnishings, and amenities are numerous and plush. For those seeking the height of Japanese luxury, the Tatami suite on the top floor is decorated in a centuries-old style that is a masterwork of delicacy and simplicity. In the Japanese-style bathroom, there's a deep bathtub for that long, slow soak at the end of a hard day. Even one's feet are tended to as terry-cloth slippers are included with robes to provide that additional Japanese touch to what already is a luxurious European extra.

Although more than a quarter of the hotel's guests are Japanese, everyone feels special here. And don't worry if you leave your inner peace at home. The Kitano will restore that to you in no time.

GUEST SERVICES: Fitness center nearby; Internet access; minibar; restaurant/bar; room service; safe in room; sound-proof windows; tea maker; TV.
NEIGHBORHOOD RESTAURANT: Salute, 270 Madison Ave. at 39th, 213-3440 (Italian brasserie with good pizzas).

Larchmont Hotel

27 West 11th Street bet. Fifth and Sixth Avenues
Phone: (212) 989-9333 Fax: (212) 989-9496
Number of Rooms: 60
Price Range: Single, $70; double, $99;
queen, $109
Credit Cards: All major
www.larchmonthotel.com

Take a right off the hustle of lower Fifth Avenue onto 11th Street, past the wrought iron fence and crenellated Gothic Revival spires of the First Presbyterian Church, and you find yourself on one of New York's loveliest and quietest landmark tree-lined streets. Walk by the turn-of-the-past-century brownstones and Greek Revival row houses and find the welcoming red door flanked by two carriage lanterns. You have arrived at the Larchmont, one of the city's newest boutique hostelries. Open the door and you are greeted by the sound of wind chimes tinkling overhead. You need to pause a second to remind yourself that you are not entering a London mews house but are standing in the center of Greenwich Village in the heart of New York City.

The Larchmont is about several things: location, perfect cleanliness, serenity, and value. The small lobby/reception area off the entryway doubles as a quiet reading lounge and is adorned with comfortable antique furniture and whimsical decorative touches. Tasteful gilded mirrors and botanical and animal prints add to the charming surroundings. Daily papers and the latest glossy magazines are casually arrayed on the upholstered ottoman.

You ascend in the creaky elevator and wind your way down the narrow halls with understated gray carpets underfoot. Each room is pleasantly decorated with rattan furnishings, ceiling fans, floral-print bedspreads, and a selection of books. Although small, they are immaculate and convey a certain hushed peacefulness. Guests are provided with a terry-cloth robe and slippers for trips to the gleaming, shared bath-

rooms. Every floor has a bright kitchenette, which stocks the basics. A free continental breakfast is served in a charming little cafe on the lower level, and the muffins are delicious.

While short on luxury, the Larchmont is long on value, and is located within a short walking distance of Washington Square Park and the best the Village has to offer.

GUEST SERVICES: Complimentary continental breakfast in café; kitchen facilities; safe; TV.

NEIGHBORHOOD RESTAURANTS: French Roast Café, 458 6th Ave. at 11th St., 533-2233 (casual, charming 24-hour French café); Japonica, 100 University Pl. at 12th St., 243-7752 (one of the best Japanese restaurants in the Village); Sammy's, 453 6th Ave. bet. 10th and 11th Sts., 924-6688 (good and casual Chinese).

Le Gamin Bed and Breakfast

132 Houston Street bet. MacDougal and Sullivan Streets
Phone: (212) 673-4592 (917) 568-3377
Fax: (212) 627-9087
www.legamin.com
b&b@legamin.com

THIS IS A LITTLE NEW YORK SECRET you should keep to yourself. Le Gamin, the hip French café mini-chain with five locations around town, has opened up a second tiny bed and breakfast on the Soho/Village border above their Soho café and around the corner from their Downing Street B&B. Only a few rooms with minimal services and amenities, this downtown "find" is for the young, cool, adventurous traveler whose idea of comfort and a good time is a café au lait, the morning paper, a warm croissant, mellow jazz on the sound system, and a warm bed upstairs.

NEIGHBORHOOD RESTAURANTS: Jane, 100 W. Houston St. between La Guardia Place and Thompson St., 254-7000 (simple menu of regional American choices in a beautiful, minimalist space); Caffe Reggio, 119 MacDougal St. between Bleecker and W. 3rd Sts., 475-9557 (oh-so-good coffees and pastries in one of Greenwich Village's original coffeehouses); Chez Jacqueline, 72 MacDougal St. between Bleecker and W. Houston Sts., 505-0727 (pretty French bistro specializing in Provençal fare).

The Library Hotel

299 Madison Avenue (at 41st Street)
Phone: (212) 983-4500 Fax: (212) 499-9099
Number of rooms: 60 rooms, 9 junior suites
Price Range: $199–$395
Credit Cards: All major
www.libraryhotel.com

THIS "PRIVATE CLUB FOR BOOKLOVERS" was opened by Henry Kallan, the force behind the nearby Hotel Giraffe. Located a block from the New York Public Library and four blocks from the Morgan Library, this boutique hotel is located in a converted turn-of-the-century office building where every floor has a different theme based on a category of knowledge. Feeling in an international mood? Book a room on the Language Floor. Got those existential blues? A room up on "Philosophy" is the thing for you. Although the overall feeling is of a cozy haven for bibliophiles, the hotel makes a great effort to make kids feel at home. For a modest extra charge, parents can call ahead and have their child's bed made up with Harry Potter, Winnie the Pooh, or Madeline sheets. Children's books are also provided. Truly a library for the whole family.

GUEST SERVICES: Business center; business video library; Internet access; complimentary breakfast; room service from nearby restaurant; passes to New York Sports Club; library.
NEIGHBORHOOD RESTAURANTS: Maeda Sushi, 16 E. 41st St. between 5th and Madison Aves., 685-4293 (top-notch sushi in serene surroundings); Bryant Park Grill, 25 W. 40th St. between 5th and 6th Aves., 840-6500 (American grill with large terrace and a strong after-work singles following).

The Lombardy

111 East 56th Street bet. Park and Lexington Avenues
Phone: (212) 753-8600 Fax: (212) 754-5683
Number of Rooms: 165
Price Range: Deluxe room, $290; two-bedroom suite, $415
Credit Cards: All major
www.lombardyhotel.com

"I LOVE YOU DARLING, but give me Park Avenue." Da-da, da-da-da . . . dunt-dunt. Eva Gabor knew what she was talking about. Well, the Lombardy isn't right on Park Avenue, but it's just a few steps off, and exudes the old-world European-style elegance to which she was referring. Built in 1926 by William Randolph Hearst, who lived here with his mistress Marion Davies, the Lombardy is a residential cooperative hotel where the units are available to the public when the owners are out of town, which happens to be most of the year.

Rooms have been individually decorated with the hotel's approval, which means you have a choice of many different

styles. The emphasis here is on luxury, calm, and quiet. Service is what you would expect in such surroundings: professional and extremely accommodating. There is a feeling of affluence in the air. The furnishings look expensive, the guests look well-heeled, carefully barbered and coiffed, and the hushed voices of the staff have a certain knowing quality. This is Fred Astaire and Ginger Rogers country.

Rooms are large and furnished to each owner's taste, so no two are alike (just think, you could stay here 165 times and never experience déjà vu). The walk-in closets are welcoming. The cool marble bathrooms and extra fluffy bath towels give a little extra comfort to the sleek surroundings. The Lombardy honors tradition, privacy, good manners, and service—qualities associated with bygone times. (When is the last time you stayed at a hotel where the staff included a seamstress?)

A few minutes' walk from the mid of Midtown, the Lombardy is ideal for business travelers and tourists alike. If you're longing for a wealthy, doting aunt who takes care of everything with style, class, and a bit of fussiness, then head to the Lombardy.

GUEST SERVICES: Business center; fitness center; parking; restaurant; room service; TV with cable and VCR.
NEIGHBORHOOD RESTAURANTS: Etoile at the Lombardy Hotel, 109 E. 56th St. bet. Park and Lexington Aves., 750-5656 (delicious American fare and after-dinner dancing); Oceana, 55 E. 54th St. bet. Madison and Park Aves., 759-5941 (wonderful seafood).

The Lowell Hotel

28 East 63rd Street bet. Madison and Park Avenues
Phone: (212) 838-1400 Fax: (212) 319-4230
Number of Rooms: 68; 48 suites
Price Range: Single, $395; deluxe two-bedroom suite, $1,425
Credit Cards: All major
www.lhw.com

THE LOWELL IS ONE OF NEW YORK'S truly exceptional lodgings and is unsurpassed in its role as the city's premier boutique hotel. If you can afford it, stay here, and forget about any place else.

Where does one start? Nestled between turn-of-the-century townhouses on a beautiful landmarked, tree-lined street on the Upper East Side, the Lowell's location is about as central as it gets. One block from Central Park. Steps from the chicest stores on Madison Avenue. A few minutes' stroll to Fifth Avenue shopping and a few minutes more to the heart of Midtown. Pass through the heavy wrought iron and

glass doors, and you enter a hallowed world of hushed elegance and sophistication. Employees are serious and proud. Is my tie straight? Is my hair combed? Everything's in the best of European tradition. *Mais bien sûr.* All the furnishings are exquisite antiques of various periods, including luxuriously upholstered chairs.

Welcome to the pages of *Architectural Digest*. Each of the 48 suites has its own character, and all have wood-burning fireplaces. For those who want to pump iron in private, book the Gym Suite with its own workout room complete with treadmill, stairmaster, ballet bar, free weights, and Nautilus. Flying in from the Left Coast? Check into the Hollywood Suite to ward off any homesickness. Or be Martha Stewart for a night and plant yourself in the Garden Suite. The Lowell is prepared to make any five-star fantasy come true.

All the accoutrements are here: the Frette robes, the Gilchrist & Soames bathroom amenities, the fresh flowers, the fully stocked bars with gourmet snacks, the book-lined shelves, and more. The Lowell anticipates your every need and desire. And at 4 P.M. you can head down to the Pembroke Room on the second floor where one of New York's fabulous afternoon teas is served. This is Edwardian elegance at its most refined.

The Lowell feels like home should feel as well as like a wonderfully luxurious escape. It is quiet, discreet, and more than a little romantic.

GUEST SERVICES: Fitness center; Internet access; minibar; restaurant/bar; room service; safe in room; tearoom; TV; valet parking.

NEIGHBORHOOD RESTAURANTS: Post House 28 E. 63rd St. bet. Park and Madison Aves., 935-2888 (comfortable and handsome steakhouse); Park Avenue Cafe, 100 E. 63rd St. at Park Ave., 644-1900 (creative American food in a sparkling setting).

Hotel Lucerne

201 West 79th Street (at Amsterdam Avenue)
Phone: (212) 875-1000 Fax: (212) 362-7251
Number of Rooms: 250
Price Range: Single, $145; king suite, $250 & up
Credit Cards: All major
www.newyorkhotel.com

A CLASSIC TURN-OF-THE-CENTURY building with a totally renovated interior, the landmarked Lucerne, reigning over the busy intersection of Amsterdam and 79th Street, is one of the newest (and oldest) and best lodging options in this part of town. One of the great pleasures in staying here, or in just walking by, for that matter, is spending a few minutes gazing at the distinguished detailing of the plum-colored brownstone and brick façade. The phrase "They don't make 'em like this anymore" couldn't be more applicable.

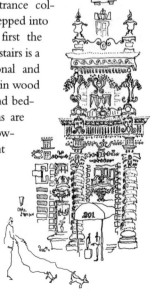

As you pass through the deeply carved and banded Baroque-style entrance columns, you feel as if you have stepped into an extravagant palace, seeing first the stylish, copper-walled lobby. Upstairs is a bit more modest, but functional and neat. Furnishings are traditional in wood and fabric, with floral drapes and bedspreads. The spotless bathrooms are of marble and granite and the towels are new and fresh. As pleasant as the rooms are, they don't quite parallel the extravagant promises made on the striking first floor. But this probably helps to keep rates as reasonable as they are.

Breakfast is served in the lobby's new Nice Matata

restaurant, which is open for lunch and dinner as well. This has become a lively neighborhood hangout.

The Lucerne's location puts it one block from the Museum of Natural History, two blocks from Central Park, and only a few minutes from Lincoln Center. The hotel is also in the heart of one of the city's most lively residential neighborhoods, and is within walking distance of hundreds of bars, restaurants, clubs, and boutiques. The Upper West Side has long wanted a good, moderately priced hotel that reflects its rich character and unique architectural history. It now has a fine one in the Lucerne.

GUEST SERVICES: Fitness center; kitchen facilities; restaurant; TV; Nintendo; jazz club; in-room movies.

NEIGHBORHOOD RESTAURANTS: Isola, 485 Columbus Ave. bet. 83rd and 84th Sts., 362-7400 (Italian trattoria); Rain, 100 W. 82nd St. at Columbus Ave., 501-0776 (delicious Pan-Asian, romantic space); Sarabeth's, 423 Amsterdam Ave. bet. 80th and 81st Sts., 496-6280 (brunch place).

The Majestic

210 West 55th Street (bet. Broadway and Seventh Avenue)
Phone: (212) 247-2000 Fax: (212) 581-2248
Number of rooms: 241 rooms; 7 suites
Price range: $149–$1500
Credit cards: All major
www.themajesticny.com

THE NAMES OF THE SUITES SAY IT ALL: Gershwin, Ellington, Astaire, Barrymore, and Sondheim—timeless creative classics with a unique, energetic personal style. This is the Majestic—a traditional yet classy boutique hotel for adults with all the modern amenities. No cascading waterfalls, theatrical staircases, or glowing hallucinogenic colors here. The lobby is comfortable and understated with only the moody euro/techno pop on the sound system and the black-and-white movies on the huge flat-screen television giving a hint of the hotel's innate hipness. Sister hotel to the fun, youthful, and happening Time Hotel on 49th Street, the Majestic opened in May 2003 and is for grownups who want a small hotel with a cool individual personality but with more comfort than attitude. Starting from the top down, the rooftop Ava Lounge evokes the spirit and style of the French Riviera in the 1950s. Think Cary Grant and Grace Kelly in *To Catch a Thief*. I can't think of a better new place to have a party in New York. Views are over to the Hudson and down into Times Square. And you're only a five-minute walk from Central Park.

Standard rooms are small, but have all the comforts and are decorated with style and care. Bathrooms have all the amenities and terry-cloth fluffiness. The larger aforementioned suites are individually decorated to evoke their namesakes: the Gershwin is festooned in rhapsodic blue comfort and the Barrymore is all Ralph Laurened in masculine woods and soothing darker tones for the plush furnishings. Situated around the corner from Carnegie Hall and the new AOL Time Warner Building and just a few minutes' walk from Times Square, the Theater District, and the gold coast shopping district of Fifth Avenue, the Majestic is perfectly located for the business traveler and tourist. And for those who just want a little taste of Cannes or Saint-Tropez among the city lights.

GUEST SERVICES: 18-hour room service; complimentary passes to outside fitness center; newspaper delivery.

NEIGHBORHOOD RESTAURANTS: Christer's, 145 W. 55th St. bet. 6th and 7th Aves., 974-7224 (rustic alpine-looking lodge serving top-notch Scandinavian fare); Taprobane, 234 W. 56th St. bet. Broadway and 8th Ave., 333-4203 (Sri Lankan with a wide variety of choices); Brooklyn Diner, 212 W. 57th St. bet. 7th Ave. and Broadway, 977-1957 (popular neighborhood diner with a decadent dessert list).

The Mansfield Hotel

12 West 44th Street bet. Fifth and Sixth Avenues
Phone: (212) 944-6050 Fax: (212) 764-4477
Number of Rooms: 124
Price Range: Standard room, $199; penthouse suite, $1369
Credit Cards: All major
www.mansfieldhotel.com

THE LOWER WEST FORTIES off Fifth Avenue is home to some of New York's most exclusive private clubs. Built around the turn-of-the-century by the greatest architectural firms of the time (McKim, Mead & White and Warren & Wetmore), the Harvard Club, the New York Yacht Club, and the Century Association are palaces of elegant old-world calm amid the chaotic crush of Midtown Manhattan. Other notable nearby establishments include the Algonquin and Royalton hotels and the Penn Club. Now add to these hallowed pantheons the Mansfield, a wonderfully charming boutique hotel built in 1906 that offers a warm, gracious welcome and a classically updated New York ambiance and style. Passing through the heavy glass doors of this neoclassical brick and stone hostelry, you enter a beautiful, small lobby that manages to be both grand and intimate. Your eyes move from the Bulgarian limestone floors to the original artwork on the walls up to the ninety-year-old moldings with illuminated brass rosettes. The salon to the right of the reception desk features a copper-domed ceiling and furniture that evokes the comfort and elegance of an earlier time. Ascend to your room either by the

grand staircase or the manually operated elevator, with its refurbished
original glass and steel doors. Alighting
at your floor, you stop suddenly: Is this
a Soho art gallery? No, but you'd be
excused for thinking so. Dark taupe
hallways, muted lighting, and stunning
black-and-white photographs create an
illusion of drama and theater. This is
New York at its best.

The small rooms have all been
renovated and decorated in the
same elegant style as the rest of the
hotel. And of course the wonderful
touches are all there: the fresh rose,
the classical CDs, the backlit head-
board, the Neutrogena amenities in the

HARPIST-PARK
STICKNEY

bathroom, the Belgian cotton bed linens and com-
forters. And what bedside would be complete without the
collected stories of Sherlock Holmes? All the extra flourish-
es show exquisite taste. Speaking of taste, that delicious smell
wafting from the hotel's kitchen is the breakfast and dessert
goodies baked on the premises.

The Mansfield is everything a wonderful small hotel in
New York should be. It has elegance, style, sophistication, and
comfort at a very reasonable price.

GUEST SERVICES: Bar; classical music recitals (Monday even-
ings); complimentary breakfast; complimentary after-theater
dessert buffet; Internet access; TV/VCR; safe in room; valet
parking; video/CD/book library.

NEIGHBORHOOD RESTAURANTS: Hatsuhana, 237 Park Ave.
at 46th St., 661-3400 (some of the best fresh sushi in town);
Osteria Al Doge, 142 W. 44th St. bet. 6th Ave. and Broadway,
944-3643 (charming Italian trattoria); Little Italy Pizza, 72 W.
45th St., 730-7575 (for a great slice of pizza).

Mayflower Hotel on the Park

15 Central Park West (at 61st Street)
Phone: (212) 265-0060 Fax: (212) 265-5098
Number of Rooms: 365
Price Range: Single, $200; park-view suite, $350
Credit Cards: All major
www.mayflowerhotel.com

Rolling hills, tree-lined paths, acres of emerald green fields, glistening ponds, baseball diamonds, a skating rink, a carousel, polar bears, sea lions, and the finish line of the New York Marathon. If you get up early enough you can even see the sun rise over the majestic apartment buildings and hotels lining Fifth Avenue. This is a view of the city most New Yorkers only dream of and one of the principal reasons for staying at the Mayflower.

This rather large, stately hotel is included in this book because its glorious location right on Central Park, and at the gateway to the Upper West Side, its big rooms with high ceilings, and its relatively low rates are features few hotels offer. Stroll through the big glass doors on Central Park West and into welcoming bustle. Is that Mickey Rourke hiding there in the corner under a big hat or Joe Pesci at the front desk? And that Valkyrie-like blonde with the violin case under her arm must be hurrying the three blocks to Lincoln Center for an eight o'clock performance. Home to many visiting movie stars, recording artists, and classical musicians, the Mayflower is a dignified, aging dowager but still a lot of fun.

And what space. What a luxurious treat to have such a big, high-ceilinged room with a walk-in closet and a spacious prewar bathroom. While the American-reproduction furniture and the flowery bedspreads have a certain dated look, I'll take light and lots of leg room over high style any day. And it's Christmas all over again when you discover the little

97

extras: kitchenettes with sinks and refrigerators, and bathroom niceties like conditioner, shampoo, sewing kit, shoe-shiner, and shower cap. Sleeping comfort is enhanced both by the princely sized firm beds and the tight security. Guests must show a key to enter the elevator, and guards with walkie-talkies monitor the lobby twenty-four hours a day.

Those in search of the ultimate I-Love-New-York experience must book one of the penthouse suites. These rooftop aeries feature terraces and balconies with views of Manhattan only a Woody Allen movie could capture. I knew that was Diane Keaton coming up in the elevator.

GUEST SERVICES: Complimentary coffee in lobby; fitness center; Internet access; refrigerators; restaurant/bar; room service; TV/VCR; valet parking.

NEIGHBORHOOD RESTAURANTS: Jean-Georges, 1 Central Park West at 60th St. and Columbus Circle, 299-3900 (luxurious atmosphere, fantastic food); Alain Ducasse, 160 Central Park South bet. 6th and 7th Aves., 265-7300 (sumptuous surroundings, four-star French cuisine in the Essex House, exorbitantly priced); Mickey Mantle's Sports Bar, 42 Central Park South bet. 5th and 6th Aves., 688-7777 (popular sports hangout with all-American food).

Melrose Hotel

140 East 63rd Street (at Lexington Avenue)
Phone: (212) 838-5700 Fax: (212) 888-4271
Number of Rooms: 310; 10 suites
Price Range: Standard double, $175; junior suite, $375
Credit Cards: All major
www.themelrosehotel.com

Now, ISN'T THIS A NICE SURPRISE. And so far a nice little secret—but not for long. Known as "New York's Most Exclusive Hotel For Young Women" since 1927, the Melrose (formerly known as Barbizon) in recent years had fallen into a state of unhappy decay and disrepair, contrasting sharply with its snappy location and former celebrity clientele, that included, albeit in their precelebrity days, the likes of Grace Kelly, Ali MacGraw, Liza Minnelli, and Candice Bergen. Then Ian Schrager bought it; then, thankfully, Metromedia, Inc. pumped in $30 million, turning the place into a charming European-style boutique hotel that is one of the nicest spots to stay on the Upper East Side.

Surrounded by elegant townhouses, the hotel is low-key and unassuming, its brick façade quietly anchoring one end of this tree-lined block. Art deco touches, marble and limestone floors, and elegant furnishings highlight the lobby, and the charming Library Bar increases the conviviality quotient considerably.

Upstairs, the hallways are clean and light, leading to midsized guest rooms that are airy and bright. As most of the neighboring buildings are five stories high, many of the rooms have pleasant views of the surrounding area and get direct sunlight. Several of the ten spectacular Tower Suites have large terraces and panoramic views. Soothing paint tones, light contemporary furniture, and Matisse prints create an overall cheery, breezy aura. Everything is brand new and spotless. It feels "just unwrapped." Rooms are equipped with all the requisite bells and whistles, and guests are given access to the adjacent 35,000-square-foot Equinox Fitness and Urban Spa, an 18-meter lap pool, and related facilities.

Three short blocks from Bloomingdale's and three and a half blocks from Central Park, with convenient access to LaGuardia and JFK airports, the Melrose is ideal for business travelers and tourists. Renovated five years ago with great care, the Melrose Hotel deserves its heartfelt recommendation.

GUEST SERVICES: Bar on premises; CD/cassette player; CD library; hair dryer in every room; laundry service; minibar; parking; room service; TV.

NEIGHBORHOOD RESTAURANTS: Brio, 786 Lexington Ave. bet. 61st and 62nd Sts., 980-2300 (tasty Italian food in relaxed setting); JoJo, 160 E. 64th St. at Lexington, 223-5656 (delicious, light, creative fare by one of New York's master chefs in a French bistro); Circus, 808 Lexington Ave. bet. 62nd and 63rd Sts., 223-2566 (cozy, fun, Brazilian with good, creative food).

The Mercer

147 Mercer Street (at Prince Street)
Phone: (212) 966-6060 Fax: 965-3838
Number of Rooms: 75
Price Range: Rooms, $325–$375;
deluxe studio, $425–$450; loft suite, $875;
courtyard loft, $1,350; penthouse suite, $2,000
Credit Cards: All major
www.themercerhotel.com

WHEN THE MERCER OPENED IN 1998, it immediately set the standard by which all new hotels will be judged. Designed by Christian Liagre, the Zen master who believes that the most important function of his work is to provide a "sense of calm in the middle of a turbulent world," the Mercer does just that. It is a spare, modern, luxurious oasis for the 21st century.

Located in the heart of Soho in an 1890 Romanesque Revival building across the street from the downtown Guggenheim Museum, the Mercer feels more like a comfortable exclusive club than a traditional hotel. No sign or marquee here; you need to know the way. The intimately scaled lobby has the hushed atmosphere of a private reading room where Soho's finest congregate. The specially designed furniture and accessories are modern in style yet plush and inviting. Upstairs,

(THE MERCER) KITCHEN

the guest rooms are modeled on the loft living pioneered in the area, with open floor plans and fifteen-foot ceilings with overhead fans. Bathrooms are spacious, with huge shower stalls and bath tubs, and the towels are thick as duvet covers. Every detail, from the rich woods and fabrics to the door handles and lighting, is designed with a Zen sense of harmony and calm. You may be in the middle of Soho, but the feeling throughout the hotel is of a soothing and serene retreat.

The Mercer is a favorite destination for the celebrity, fashion, and film crowd and has already been host to the likes of Leonardo DiCaprio, Cher, and Calvin Klein. The hotel restaurant, Mercer Kitchen, features one of New York's greatest chefs, Jean-Georges Vongerichten, and is packed nightly. Cappuccino and croissants in the street-level cafe are as close to a power breakfast as you can get in Soho. At the Mercer, the stars are definitely in alignment for one of New York's great hotel experiences.

GUEST SERVICES: CD player; bar on premises; fitness center; restaurant; room service; TV with cable and VCR.

NEIGHBORHOOD RESTAURANTS: Mercer Kitchen, 99 Prince St. at Mercer St., 966-5454 (creative fare in subterranean space); Zoe, 90 Prince St., bet. Mercer St. and Broadway, 966-6722 (delicious Californian cuisine in stunning airy space); Cub Room and Cub Room Cafe, 131 Sullivan St. at Prince St., 677-4100 (wonderful new American cuisine in beautiful dining room with a happening bar).

Hotel Metro

45 West 35th Street bet. Fifth and Sixth Avenues
Phone: (212) 947-2500 Fax: (212) 279-1310
Reservations: (800) 356-3870
Number of Rooms: 170
Price Range: Single, $145–$225; double, $155–$250;
two-bedroom family room, $200–$225
Credit Cards: All major
www.hotelmetronyc.com

SINATRA ON THE SOUND SYSTEM. Art deco every-where. The Empire State Building around the corner. Ahhhhh, New York, New York. Welcome to the Hotel Metro, an independent European-style boutique hotel in the Macy's/Herald Square/Madison Square Garden/ Penn Station/ garment district area.

Built in 1901, this historic building recently under-went a complete interior renovation and opened as the Metro in April 1995. Style and value are paramount here. Hollywood publicity photos and movie posters complement deco furnishings and decorative details to give the spacious public rooms a sleek, whimsi-cal look. Grab a book off the library shelf and relax by the fireplace with a glass of wine in the evening, or take your time over breakfast and the daily papers in the comfortable lounge. These are hotel spaces in which you may want to linger.

Upstairs, the largish rooms carry on the art deco theme. Furnishings are modest but tasteful. Closets are ample, and an iron and ironing board are provid-ed. Bathroom towels are luxu-riously thick and comfy.

A wonderful surprise is the big rooftop terrace with an inspiring view of the Empire State Building—a glorious benefit if you stay during warm weather. The area immediately surrounding the hotel is a bit dark and dreary, but some of the best Korean restaurants in the city are nearby, as are many major tourist attractions. Prices at the Metro are relatively low, putting this hotel close to the "find" and "good deal" categories. It may not be well known or in the fanciest part of town, but it's worth discovering.

GUEST SERVICES: Complimentary breakfast; Internet access; fitness center; restaurant/bar; room service; safe on premises; TV.

NEIGHBORHOOD RESTAURANTS: Keen's Chop House, 72 W. 36th St. bet. 5th and 6th Aves., 947-3636 (classic 1885 saloon with solid American food); Won Jo, 23 W. 32nd St. bet. 5th Ave. and Broadway, 695-5815 (all-night Korean barbecue); Bienvenue Restaurant, 21 E. 36th St. bet. 5th and Madison Aves., 684-0215 (small, fun French bistro with good, low-priced fare).

Morgans

237 Madison Avenue bet. 37th and 38th Streets
Phone: (212) 686-0300 Fax: (212) 779-8352
Number of Rooms: 154
Price Range: Single, $205; double, $230;
suite, $415; penthouse, $2,000
Credit Cards: All major
www.ianschragerhotels.com

YOU DON'T HAVE TO BE A MOVIE STAR to get a room at Morgans, but staying here will certainly make you feel like one. Hip, ultra-chic, and owned by Ian Schrager of Studio 54 fame (also the hotelier of the Royalton and the Paramount), Morgans was one of the first of the designer boutique hotels in New York. Since its opening, it has been home to many visiting movie stars, celebrities, and media and fashion executives, and it's easy to tell why. The cool, minimalist design by the French designer, Andrée Putman, and her evident attention to every small aspect of the hotel, is intoxicating. Everything seems endowed with a sense of understated glamour and anticipated drama. From the silver-tipped matches in the custom-made matchboxes to the Kiehl's lotion in the bathrooms—no detail is overlooked. And where do they get that black sand for the hall ashtrays? Australia?

The doormen—young, attractive model types—stand sentry at the entrance to the lobby, a chic urban lounge with plush deco leather armchairs, an Escher-like carpet, fresh orchids, designer lamps, and recessed spots for the perfect theatrical lighting effect: "Mr. De Mille, I'm ready for my close-up."

Rooms are small but so beautifully and carefully designed you hardly notice. The uncluttered Japanese-like spaces are oases of calm and peace, their soft ecru and gray color schemes at once pleasing and soothing. And what's that sound? Nothing, absolutely nothing. Double-paned windows and a quiet Murray Hill location ensure soporific sounds of silence.

In many ways Morgans is the quintessential boutique hotel: small, beautiful, well-priced, and infused with enough drama and theatrical effects to give you a little extra high New York style. You don't have to be a Brad Pitt or a Julia Roberts to stay here, but don't be surprised if you see them in the hall.

GUEST SERVICES: Complimentary breakfast; bar on premises, CD players; minibar; restaurant (Asia de Cuba—one of the hottest new restaurants in town serving Asian/Latin fusion cuisine); fitness center; TV with cable.

NEIGHBORHOOD RESTAURANTS: Stella del Mare, 346 Lexington Ave. bet. 39th and 40th Sts., 687-4425 (elegant and romantic Italian seafooder); Water Club, 500 E. 30th St. at the East River, 683-3333 (stunning views, top seafood); Oyster Bar, E. 42nd St. in Grand Central Station, lower level, 490-6650 (New York seafood institution).

Murray Hill East Suites

149 East 39th Street bet. Lexington and Third Avenues
Phone: (800) 248-9999, (212) 661-2100
Fax: (212) 818-0724
Number of Rooms: 120
Price Range: Studio suite, $179;
two-bedroom suite, $499; monthly rates available
Credit Cards: All major

THERE ARE NEIGHBORHOODS IN NEW YORK we rarely seem to visit for one reason or another. Maybe they consist mostly of office buildings. Or maybe there's just not that much going on to draw you there. Murray Hill has a reputation as one of these areas. Other than the Morgan Library on Madison Avenue and 36th Street, there is nothing here that could be considered a destination. And therein lies its appeal. It's quiet. It's unassuming. It's off the beaten track. It feels like a true residential neighborhood where passersby greet each other on the street (I actually saw a man doff his hat), and there is still a Greek deli on the corner and a shoe repair man who has been just around the block for years. These are the principal reasons for staying at the Murray Hill East Suites. The fact that accommodations are all suites, each with a kitchenette, and at very affordable prices also makes this hotel a wise choice for business travelers and visiting families. Staying here is like having your own little pied-à-terre in the city.

Coming into the lobby, down a few steps under the green front awning, you'd never guess you were entering a hotel. The friendly, uniformed doorman holds the door while giving you a knowing nod. You already feel welcome. The décor is somewhat corporate: it's all clean, efficient, and unthreatening. You know there aren't going to be any unpleasant surprises. Upstairs the purple and green color schemes take a little getting used to, but the rooms are decently sized and spotless, with suitable furnishings. Pack what you will, as closets are roomy and there are plenty of wooden hangers. Ask for a room on one of the upper floors so that you might have a glimpse of the East River or the Empire State Building.

The Murray Hill East Suites deliver just what they promise: roomy, tidy, comfortable accommodations at a reasonable price. It's just a pleasant, welcoming home in a nice quiet neighborhood. A destination worth heading for.

GUEST SERVICES: Kitchen facilities; TV with cable.
NEIGHBORHOOD RESTAURANTS: Park Bistro, 414 Park Ave. South bet. 28th and 29th Sts., 689-1360 (updated French bistro cooking with Provençal flair); Tatany, 380 3rd Ave. bet. 27th and 28th Sts., 686-1871 (bustling Japanese restaurant with good sushi).

The Muse

130 West 46th Street bet. Fifth and Sixth Avenues
Phone: (212) 485-2400 Fax: (212) 485-2900
Number of Rooms: 200; 2 grand suites; 14 junior suites
Price Range: $199–$449
Credit Cards: All major
www.themusehotel.com

TAKE PICASSO'S "THE JAZZ PLAYERS," MIX in Louis Armstrong's "Potato Head Blues," add a dash of luxurious post-modern design and you have a hint of what is served up at The Muse, a new, upscale boutique hotel in the Theater District. Taking inspiration from its surroundings, The Muse celebrates Broadway and the performing arts in every detail. Spacious, comfortable rooms are furnished in cool, contemporary style, accented with splashes of color, as with the thick duvets on every bed. For meditative pursuits, bedside tables are equipped with scented candles and miniature rock gardens. Marble bathrooms offer all the little extras—an orchid here, luxury soaps and thick towels there. If you want to be in or near the Theater District, this hotel is an excellent choice.

GUEST SERVICES: In-room spa services; fitness center; room service; Philosophy amenities; hair dryers; cordless telephones; coffee makers; Internet access; safe; minibar.

NEIGHBORHOOD RESTAURANTS: District, 130 W. 46th St. bet. 6th and 7th Aves., 485-2999 (New American fare in a calm oasis); Café Un Deux Trois, 123 W. 44th St. between 6th and 7th Aves., 354-4148 (large, popular French brasserie that's good for kids); Bread from Beirut, 24 W. 45th St. between 5th and 6th Aves., 764-1588 (good but casual Lebanese takeout).

Paramount

235 West 46th Street bet. Seventh and Eighth Avenues
Phone: (212) 764-5500 Fax: (212) 575-2196
Number of Rooms: 610
Price Range: Single, $125–$255; two-bedroom suite, $460
Credit Cards: All major
www.ianschragerhotels.com

No SIGN. NO STREET NUMBER. The message is clear: if you can find it, you must be the kind of person who knows where to go in New York. Minimalist, attitude rich, and just a few well-heeled steps off Times Square, the Paramount is *the* hip hotel.

Owner Ian Schrager, the undisputed high priest of chic hostelry, and über-designer Philippe Starck have created the hotel of the see-and-be-seen crowd. This is lobby with drama, comedy, and intrigue. The jagged grand stairway beckons you to the mezzanine lounge/restaurant. Settle into one of the lobby's curvaceous velvet upholstered chairs and take in the fanciful art deco surroundings in stunning oranges, greens, yellows and violets—colors that serve as the design leitmotif throughout the hotel. The adjacent bar, The Paramount Bar, is a buzzing scene. The Dean & Deluca espresso bar and deluxe gourmet shop caters to the milling throngs of visiting swells and local sophisticates. Even the bathrooms are a triumph of flair, style, and humor.

With its air of whimsy, the Paramount manages to be both hip and great for children. The most family-friendly of Schrager's New York hotels, it boasts a playroom designed by Gary Panter (the artist behind Pee-wee Herman's TV playhouse) and features glorious animal-shaped chairs.

Head upstairs and be greeted by the day's weather illuminated on the hallway wall as you get off the elevator. Room numbers are barely suggested atop the doors. Tiny single rooms are devoid of decoration but for a looming enlargement of Vermeer's "The Lacemaker" above the bed. Everything oozes high style, from the high-backed velour chairs to the suspended light fixture over the desk to the black-and-gray checked carpet. Luxurious linens and daily fresh flowers fairly guarantee a restful, comforting stay.

The Paramount is New York's grand hotel with an attitude. It is an art deco dream that is fun, beautiful, mischievous, and great for all ages. New York in a nutshell.

GUEST SERVICES: Fitness center; restaurant; room service; TV with cable and VCR; video library.

NEIGHBORHOOD RESTAURANTS: Orso, 322 W. 46th St. bet. 8th and 9th Aves., 489-7212 (cozy, comfortable, excellent Italian); Joe Allen, 326 W. 46th St. bet. 8th and 9th Aves., 581-6464 (classic American with checkered tablecloths; popular with theater crowd); Jezebel, 630 9th Ave. at 45th St., 582-1045 (unique bordello atmosphere, great southern-soul food).

Park South Hotel

122 E.ast 28th Street between Park and Lexington Avenues
Phone: (212) 448-0888 Fax: (212) 448-0811
Number of rooms: 143
Price range: $209–$325
Credit Cards: All major
www.parksouthhotel.com
Susana@parksouthhotel.com

TUCKED ONTO A NONDESCRIPT SIDE STREET IN Curry Hill (named for its Indian shops and restaurants) and just a few blocks north of Gramercy Park, this eight-story hotel is located in a restored historic 1906 building. Opened on September 9, 2001, the Park South exudes classic New York style, yet offers the latest in high-tech amenities and furnishings. The handsome uniformed doorman greets you with a smile and ushers you into the quiet, understated lobby. Didn't you just see him in a Ralph Lauren ad? You can tell the hotel's decorator was working with a modest budget, but had lots of style, taste, and class. Sink into the big leather sofa and look around for a moment. Art nouveau touches and simple elegant furnishings create a soothing oasis for the tired traveler. Everything is exceptionally clean, and the hotel staff is incredibly friendly and helpful, giving the Park South the ambiance of a private club where you are known and cared for. The bedrooms are smallish, but comfortable. Numerous stylish elements give the feeling of a little more than your normal standard bedroom. I particularly liked the wooden headboards and the black-and-white photos of old New York.

The hotel attracts a business clientele as well as tourists who want to be downtown but also within walking distance of Midtown. While not at all chic or trendy, the Park South is a classic, attractive, clean and moderately priced boutique hotel that is just a little bit off the beaten track. How nice to find a quiet, welcoming little spot that you can call your own.

112 BEST LITTLE HOTELS

GUEST SERVICES: On-site cardiovascular fitness room, cable TV.

NEIGHBORHOOD RESTAURANTS: Blue Smoke, 116 E. 27th St. bet. Lexington and Park Aves., 447-7733 (casual BBQ joint by entrepreneur Danny Meyer, which translates to terrific food and top-notch service in a beautiful space); I Trulli, 122 E. 27th St., bet. Lexington and Park Aves., 481-7372 (Italian wine bar with lots of choices by the glass and tasty Tuscan snacks); Annapurna, 108 Lexington Ave. bet. 27th and 28th Sts., 679-1284 (a great Curry Hill standout).

The Premier

145 West 44th Street bet. Sixth Avenue and Broadway
Phone: (212) 768-4400 Fax: (212) 768-0847
Reservations: (800) 622-5569
Number of Rooms: 125
Price Range: Studio (queen), $395; grand (king), $495
Credit Cards: All major
www.millenniumhotels.com

JUST OFF TIMES SQUARE STANDS THE PREMIER, 21 floors of steel and glass—a sleek, post-modern luxury boutique hotel offering the latest in accommodations and amenities in a bright, luminous setting. Catering to the corporate traveler wanting something special and to the upscale tourist looking for a small European-style hotel near the theaters and Midtown, the Premier is for those who care more about comfort, peace, and luxury than trendy fashion and designer furnishings. The staff at the Premier anticipates all your needs and fulfills them in a professional, efficient way.

Walk into the double-height lobby and you're greeted by a large '30s WPA-style mural that is part Diego Rivera, part Balthus, exuding the energy and style that is New York. The Premier has contemporary furniture, dramatic track lighting, and floor-to-ceiling windows with stunning views of the surrounding area. This is a boutique hotel for our times. Fresh flowers are everywhere: a bouquet of tulips greets you as you get off at your floor. Every nook seems to contain a sensuous orchid. Hall walls are lined with contemporary New York photographs. The modern rooms are filled with bright, cheery colors and unexpected treats: gourmet food baskets, trays of various teas, and more flowers adorning the desk. Beds and pillows are deliciously comfortable and welcoming. Tubs are deep and long. The nightly turn-down service comes with fresh slippers and little flower petals on the pillow. You just want to sink in and stay.

Feeling hungry at any hour? The 24-hour second-floor lounge offers a changing menu of tasty delights: Continental breakfast in the morning, sandwiches, fruit and pastries in the afternoon, and wine and hors d'oeuvres at night. And don't forget to try their signature champagne popsicle, made exclusively for the hotel. The Premier is a wonderful alternative to the nearby large tourist hotels for those wanting to stay in the Times Square area and yet escape to an oasis of serenity and luxury.

GUEST SERVICES: Fitness center; hair dryers; minibar; laundry service; parking; room service; TV with cable.

NEIGHBORHOOD RESTAURANTS: Johnnie's, 135 W. 45th bet. 6th Ave. and Broadway, 869-5565 (small, old-world Italian); Charlotte, 145 W. 44th St. bet. 6th Ave. and Broadway, 768-7508 (new-American cuisine in understated corporate setting); Langan's Bar and Restaurant, 150 W. 47th St. bet. 6th and 7th Aves. 869-5482 (pleasant pub with American/Continental fare and lively action at the bar).

Regent Wall Street

55 Wall Street (bet. William Street and Hanover Square)
Phone: (212) 845-8600 Fax: (212) 845-8601
Number of Rooms: 144; 47 suites
Price Range: $395–$995
Credit Cards: All major
www.regentshotels.com
rwreservations@regentshotels.com

THIS PALATIAL HOTEL, LOCATED IN a monumental Greek Revival landmark building (formerly the 1842 Mercantile Exchange), is nothing less than awe-inspiring. It might be a turn-of-the-century private club for European aristocracy, with its jaw-dropping architectural details that include a three-story-high domed main hall, eighteen soaring Ionic columns, and an 80-foot, elliptical copper-domed roof. Persian rugs and marble floors abound. Rooms are large, comfortable, and exquisitely decorated. A perfect spot for affluent business travelers with a taste for Golden Age ambiance.

GUEST SERVICES: Fitness center; Internet access; room service; spa; two-line telephone; TV/DVD, restaurant/lounge/bar.
NEIGHBORHOOD RESTAURANTS: Delmonico's, 56 Beaver St. at William St., 509-1144 (upscale, elegant American); Stone Street Tavern, 52 Stone St. bet. South William and Broad Sts., 425-3663 (19th-century eatery filled with history and nostalgia).

Roger Smith Hotel

501 Lexington Avenue (at 47th Street)
Phone: (212) 755-1400 Fax: (212) 758-4061
Number of Rooms: 136
Price Range: Single, $240; suites, $295
Credit Cards: All major
www.rogersmith.com

HOTEL AS GALLERY. BUILDING AS SCULPTURE. Staff members as artisans toiling in happy, creative harmony. A utopian cultural haven in Midtown Manhattan for those of a fine artistic bent. This is the vision owner/proprietor/chief artist-in-residence James Knowles seeks in his specialty boutique hotel.

Here art rules and is omnipresent. Rotating exhibits adorn the hallways. The walls of the bar and restaurant have been playfully painted by Mr. Knowles's own hand, and the lobby serves as a gallery for his abstract bronzes, life-sized busts, and oil paintings. The Roger Smith is a charming small hotel that reflects the spirit and personality of its owner.

A recent renovation was executed with an artist's eye and respect for materials and details. Corridors are wide and well lit with mahogany millwork and the works of whatever artist is currently being featured. The 136 rooms are comfortably large, each one surprisingly different with individually chosen furnishings and custom-made curtains. Wooden hangers are ample; down pillows are available upon request, and five sumptuous towels await you after your shower. Available reading material ranges from Jackie Collins to James Joyce, with the requisite art book always at hand.

In keeping with his effort to make the Roger Smith for the visual arts what

117

the Algonquin once was to literature, Mr. Knowles holds weekly meetings in the penthouse. Featured lecturers include artists, art critics, and the occasional chefs who are guests of the hotel. The Roger Smith is closer in spirit to the Royalton, Morgans, and the Paramount than to its more buttoned-down neighbors. It is whimsical, yet comfortable. Mr. Knowles has found a niche for his very personal hotel. In a city where artistic creativity is central to its identity and vibrancy, there clearly is room and need for such a vision.

GUEST SERVICES: Complimentary breakfast; coffee makers in rooms; minibar; restaurant with bar; room service; TV with cable; complimentary movie rentals; offsite health club; VIP car service.

NEIGHBORHOOD RESTAURANTS: Sparks, 210 E. 46th St. bet. 2nd and 3rd Aves., 687-4855 (one of NY's great steakhouses, great wine list); Kuruma Zushi, 7 E. 47th St. bet. 5th and Madison Aves., 317-2802 (expensive and superb); Comfort Diner, 214 E. 45th St. bet. 2nd and 3rd Aves., 867-4555 (retro fifties diner with good American fare); Diwan, 148 E. 48th St. bet. Lexington and 3rd Aves., 593-5425 (elegant Indian restaurant).

The Roger Williams Hotel

131 Madison Avenue (at 31st Street)
Phone: (212) 448-7000 Fax: (212) 448-7007
Number of Rooms: 180
Price Range: Single or double, $255
Credit Cards: All major
www.rogerwilliamshotel.com

IF YOU WANT TO STAY IN THE MURRAY HILL area, the Roger Williams should definitely be on your short list of hotels to consider. This establishment defines the meaning of a charming, quiet little boutique hotel. The reasonable rates, elegant décor, and handsome, helpful staff add to its winsome appeal.

Walk through the huge glass doors and you enter an oversized pillared lobby with 20-foot ceilings. Cool limestone walls and subtle statuary provide tasteful accents. Everything feels just right—created with an aesthetic eye for style and detail. The greenish clay-colored hallways are set off by gentle lighting to create a soothing, relaxed atmosphere. The rooms are of various sizes and all of them are very comfortable. They feel light and airy and are enhanced by blond wood furnishings and white Japanese screens. The emphasis here is more on mood and atmosphere than on space and pretentiousness. Bathrooms are beige marble with steel fixtures and all the little amenities are on hand. The Roger Williams provides a complimentary video and CD library, well-chosen bedside reading material, complimentary mineral water, and delicious continental breakfasts and afternoon teas.

Prices are relatively low, rates you would normally pay for basic accommodations with very few extras. Yet the Roger Williams has created an aura of simplicity and taste while including the comfortable and artistic touches that truly matter. This place feels special, as if someone really cares about it. There is no question that when staying here, you will feel special, too.

GUEST SERVICES: Complimentary breakfast; CD and video library; CD players; complimentary coffee/tea, TV with VCR.

NEIGHBORHOOD RESTAURANTS: Artisanal, 2 Park Avenue South at 32nd St., 725-8585 (Terrance Brennan's homage to artisanal cheeses), Hangawi, 12 E. 32nd St. bet. 5th Avenue and Madison Avenues, 213-0077 (Korean vegetarian in a serene, elegant space).

Rooms to Let

83 Horatio Street (at Washington Street)
Phone: (212) 675-5481 Fax: (212) 675-9432
Number of Rooms: 4
Price Range: $95–$135, minimum stay is 4 nights;
private apartment, prices on request
Credit Cards: None
www.roomstolet.net

AN 1852 GREEK REVIVAL TOWNHOUSE on a beautiful quiet street in the way West Village is the site of this homey and comfortable bed and breakfast. Its quirky name harks back to the age of cobblestone streets, horsedrawn carriages, and gas-lit street lamps. Today you're likely to see the lights of the Empire State Building as you look out from the charming back garden, or you might catch a glimpse of a passing ocean liner as you watch the sun set over the Hudson River from the front stoop. Nonetheless, time has moved slowly at the Rooms to Let B&B, and to stay in one of the four cozy rooms is to feel gently cossetted and removed from the normal frantic pace of New York. Take a book and a cup of coffee and sink into one of the comfortable chairs in the front parlor or nap in the hammock in the garden if the weather is warm.

Proprietor and local artist Marjorie Colt pretty much gives you the run of the place and leaves you alone. Her only rule is that the first guest down in the morning starts the coffee maker. The eclectic furnishings—a hodgepodge of grandmother's antiques, miscellaneous tchotchkes, country quilts, and area rugs—evoke a familiar feeling of home. Decorations are primarily paintings by the owner. Rooms are smallish but pleasant and bright, and the old-fashioned paned windows accented by lace panel curtains add a charming period touch. What a treat to stand at those windows and look out through the trees to the quiet street below. It's a great place to daydream. Try to get one of the rooms with a fireplace—they are beautiful to look at even when not in use. Bathrooms are shared but are very clean.

Rooms to Let feels remote and out-of-the-way but is only minutes from the heart of Greenwich Village, Soho, and Chelsea. Its relatively low rates, along with its friendly, personal, and somewhat quirky hominess, make it a particularly attractive getaway. If you click your ruby slippers together and say "There's no place like home" you're likely to end up at 83 Horatio Street. (Gee, Toto . . .)

GUEST SERVICES: Continental breakfast.
NEIGHBORHOOD RESTAURANTS: Frank's, 85 10th Ave. at 15th St., 243-1349 (meat-packing district steakhouse); Florent, 69 Gansevoort St. bet. Greenwich and Washington Sts., 989-5779 (popular French bistro/diner with cool clientele); Hog Pit, 22 9th Ave. at 13th St., 604-0092 (BBQ with jukebox).

Royalton

44 West 44th Street bet. Fifth and Sixth Avenues
Phone: (212) 869-4400 Fax: (212) 869-8965
Number of Rooms: 205
Price Range: Single, $275; suite, $415
Credit Cards: All major
www.ianschragerhotels.com

THE ROYALTON IS ONE of New York's early designer boutique hotels, and as the centerpiece in Ian Schrager's hotel empire it continues to be a designated landmark on the city's list of ultra-hip destinations. As with all Schrager hotels, the style quotient is high, the interiors and furnishings beautifully designed by Philippe Starck, and the staff famous for both its beauty and attitude. This is a place about drama and cutting-edge décor created for those who live in New York as well as those who visit.

Once you pass through the intimidating entrance, you enter a fantastic world. If nightclubs and discotheques were the New York hangouts of the '70s, hotel lobbies are the quintessential gathering places now, and the Royalton's lobby is just that. Yards of cobalt blue carpet lead you Oz-like through the slate gray bilevel lobby, past intimate seating areas of cushy club chairs and sofas covered in miles of white fabric, paired with African and Chinese ottomans. The overall effect is stunning and bold. Here fashion, media, Hollywood, and publishing types mix with sophisticated visitors and in-the-know locals for drinks and gossip in a vanity fair of style and posing. And should you need further amusement, there are tables set for impromptu games of checkers, chess, dominoes, and Chinese checkers. (And don't miss the public bathrooms: yes, look behind the mirrored wall.)

For a respite, check into your room, where a passion for feeling and texture predominate. Larger rooms feature working fireplaces, five-foot round custom tubs built into concave slate walls or slate-and-glass-walled showers, cushioned

window seats, and triangle-shaped Italian-cut glass vanities. Call down to the front desk for a video, and it's delivered with a bowl of warm popcorn.

A stay at the Royalton is a truly New York experience and just a few minutes in the lobby, a meal at 44, or a drink at the Round Bar will confirm this. These are all A-list destinations, and going stronger than ever. If that looks like Calvin Klein seated at one of the banquette tables along the wall, that's because it is.

The Royalton is about having fun, about seeing and being seen. It's about feeling and looking chic and drinking a big, expensive martini in glowing, sophisticated surroundings and watching all the beautiful people float by. It's about New York at its coolest and most elegant.

GUEST SERVICES: Cassette players; working fireplaces (in some rooms); fitness center; minibar; restaurant with bar; room service; conference capability; TV with cable and VCR. NEIGHBORHOOD RESTAURANTS: Chikubu 12 E. 44th St. at 5th Ave., 818-0715 (excellent Japanese restaurant); Jewel of India, 15 W. 44th St. bet. 5th and Sixth Aves., 869-5544 (great Tandoori dishes in deluxe setting); Torre di Pisa, 19 W. 44th St. bet 5th and 6th Aves., 398-4400 (top Tuscan food, great décor, cigar room).

The Shoreham Hotel

33 West 55th Street bet. Fifth and Sixth Avenues
Phone: (212) 247-6700 Fax: (212) 765-9741
Number of Rooms: 176
Price Range: Double, $235; suites, $325 & up
Credit Cards: All major
www.shorehamhotel.com

AN INTIMATE, BEAUTIFULLY DESIGNED boutique
hotel at affordable prices just off the choicest part of Fifth
Avenue, the Shoreham is elegant, low-key, and quiet—
perfect for the repeat guests who comprise most of their corporate clientele. The sleek minimalist style in this standard
bearer of the unique almost belies the friendly service that
greets the weary traveler.

This is the kind of hotel you would create for yourself
if you had designer taste and a modest budget. Special touches abound: fresh lilies on the Jay Spectre glass coffee tables
surrounded by brushed steel and leather armchairs, recessed
lighting, original futuristic canvases by Winold Reiss, and
black-and-white marble floors. The lobby, although small,
both welcomes and impresses.

Upstairs, the emphasis is on comfort. With back-lit per-
forated metal headboards, the beds seem to glow as they

beckon you with soft, downy pillows and thick duvets. Sitting room and bedroom areas in the suites are divided by opalescent glass and steel panels that echo the elegance and airiness evident throughout the hotel. While the rooms are small, deluxe touches like cedar closets, the fresh rose by your bed, a personal library, and the cool, well-appointed bathroom will seduce you nonetheless.

The Shoreham is centrally located, reasonably priced, lovely to look at, and offers a restful stay.

GUEST SERVICES: Complimentary breakfast; CD player; complimentary dessert buffet; free Bailey's fitness center; hair dryer in every room; laundry services; discount valet parking; refrigerators; TV with VCR.

NEIGHBORHOOD RESTAURANTS: La Côte Basque, 60 W. 55th St. bet. 5th and 6th Aves., 688-6525 (superb, classic French restaurant); Michael's, 24 W. 55th St. bet. 5th and 6th Aves., 767-0555 (delicious Californian cuisine in artful surroundings); Allegria, 1350 6th Ave., entrance on 55th St. bet. 5th and 6th Aves., 956-7755 (casual, snappy pizzeria-trattoria).

60 Thompson

60 Thompson Street bet. Spring and Broome Streets
Phone: (212) 431-0400 Fax: (212) 431-0200
Number of Rooms: 100, including 10 suites
Price Range: Single: $370, deluxe room: $395,
suite: $450, Presidential suite: $3,500
Credit cards: All major
www.60thompson.com
lhenao@60Thompson.com

THIS IS ONE OF NEW YORK'S GREAT new boutique hotels and quintessentially Soho: cool, hip, and minimalist but also very cozy and homey. Although newly constructed, it has the look and feel of a sedate residential building. It caters to young professionals in the arts and media, sort of a private club for the bicoastal crowd. Nestled on a charming side street dotted with galleries, restaurants, and boutiques, it blends in seamlessly with its surroundings. You'd never guess it was a hotel, except for the presence of young doormen in their understated uniforms. On the second floor, the "living room" is the place to relax in cushy armchairs while reading the *Financial Times*. Bedrooms, soothingly designed, are replete with comforting luxuries like Frette linens, Philosophy toiletries, and Dean & Deluca–stocked minibars. Many have sweeping views over Soho and beyond. Thom, the hotel's adjacent restaurant, is one of the most happening restaurants on the downtown dining scene.

GUEST SERVICES: Internet access; restaurant; rooftop garden; lounge; DVD, CD in every room.

NEIGHBORHOOD RESTAURANTS: Bistro Les Amis, 180 Spring St. at Thompson St., 226-8645 (charming, flower-filled French bistro); Britti Caffe, 110 Thompson St. bet. Spring and Prince Sts., 334-6604 (cozy neighborhood spot with good selection of Italian bites and great cocktail list); Kin Khao, 171 Spring St. bet. Thompson St. and West Broadway, 966-3939 (trendy, always-crowded Thai).

Sofitel

45 West 44th Street bet. Fifth and Sixth Avenues
Phone: (212) 354-8844 Fax: (212) 354-2480
www.sofitel.com
Number of Rooms: 398, including 52 executive suites
Price Range: Single rooms: $199; suites: $529

SOFITEL HOTELS & RESORTS, the renowned French hotel chain, brings a little bit of Paris to Midtown Manhattan. Opened, appropriately enough, on Bastille Day, July 2000, the newly constructed Sofitel New York has been designed with the upscale business traveler in mind, serving up all the expected luxuries and amenities. Though rather grand in scale—it occupies 29 stories—the Sofitel has an intimate feel, owing to the art deco design and generally comfortable surroundings amply furnished with overstuffed sofas and leather club chairs. Rooms are large and many have great city views. The oversized bathrooms feature roomy glass-enclosed showers and separate tubs, with Roger & Gallet toiletries completing the pretty, French-style picture. While not exactly hip, the Sofitel is not the least bit stuffy either. It's simply a serious hotel for the serious traveler.

GUEST SERVICES: Bakery; business meeting facilities with video conferencing; fitness center; gift shop; Internet access. NEIGHBORHOOD RESTAURANTS: Angus McIndoe, 258 W. 44th St. bet. Broadway and 8th Ave., 221-9222 (celebrity-studded American spot); Carmine's, 200 W. 44th St. bet. 5th and 6th Aves., 221-3800 (family-style Italian that's good for groups); DB Bistro Moderne, 55 W. 44th St. bet. 5th and 6th Aves., 391-2400 (Daniel Boulud's terrific, albeit pricey, bistro).

Soho Bed and Breakfast

167 Crosby Street at Bleecker Street
Phone: (212) 925-1034 Fax: (212) 925-1034
Number of Rooms: 2; The Townhouse B&B (hosted),
The Carriage House (unhosted)
Price Range: 1–2 days, $125; 3 days and more, $100 (single),
$125 (double); 3 persons, $160; 4 persons, $200
Credit Cards: None
www.citysonnet.com

IF YOU EVER WANTED TO STAY in a Greenwich Village loft and live the downtown bohemian life, Gary Rich, the charming and garrulous host of Soho Bed and Breakfast, will make this dream come true.

Located in a townhouse and an adjacent carriage house built in 1792, the Soho B&B (actually in Greenwich Village) is located above the Bleecker Street Tavern and across the street from New York's first skyscraper (Louis Sullivan's Condict Building, built in 1898). The space has two separate accommodations: a huge, high-ceilinged loft and a carriage house, both of which include kitchen facilities, dining and sitting areas, and a master bedroom. These are very personal spaces, mirroring the eclectic tastes of your host. Fans hang from the beamed ceilings. Huge abstract paintings adorn the brick walls. Tribal art and masks are hung beside Rich's cricket bat and framed foreign currency. Dusty books lean tiredly in their shelves, and found objects are everywhere. This is loft-as-museum, room-as-art gallery, apartment-as–flea market. (Ask Mr. Rich for a view of his motorcycle collection in the back garage. Everything is for sale, and that vintage Vespa looks like the perfect way to weave through the crowded Soho streets.)

The Soho Bed and Breakfast is for those seeking an authentic downtown experience. Once Mr. Rich hands over your front-door key, you're a local. Walk a half block to lower Broadway, and there's Tower Records and NYU students galore. Or head around the corner to the Public Theater and St. Mark's Place, gateway to the East Village.

Come prepared: Crosby Street is narrow and might look like a dark alley. The front door is covered with graffiti. There is no elevator, and it's a one-flight walk up to the carriage house and three to the loft. Pack a sense of humor and adventure. This is downtown New York.

GUEST SERVICES: Kitchen facilities; TV with cable and VCR. NEIGHBORHOOD RESTAURANTS: Temple Bar, 332 Lafayette St. at Bleecker St., 925-4242 (hot spot where you go more for the drinks than the food); Bond St., 6 Bond St. bet. Broadway and Lafayette St., 777-2500 (excellent Japanese in stylish setting); Savoy, 70 Prince St. at Crosby St., 219-8570 (charming and cozy serving new American fare; several fireplaces).

Soho Grand Hotel

310 West Broadway bet. Canal and Grand Streets
Phone: (212) 965-3000 Fax: (212) 334-7597
Number of Rooms: 367
Price Range: Double, $289; penthouse suite, $1,000 and up
Credit Cards: All major
www.sohogrand.com

RISING FIFTEEN STORIES above its diminutive cast iron neighbors, the Soho Grand attempts to re-create in Soho what the Royalton and Paramount have accomplished in Midtown. By offering modern style and chic atmosphere at moderate prices, it attracts a cool and trendy mix of artists, models, and fashion and entertainment types, who, in turn, attract the visitors in search of them. It's a great formula for success, and it appears to be working splendidly since the Soho Grand opened its doors in 1996.

Pass through an understated entryway, and enter a realm of industrial chic, designed to reflect the famous cast iron architecture of the neighborhood. A grand suspended steel staircase embedded with bottle glass of the kind once used to light workshops below street level leads you to an even grander lobby. The soaring space radiates the aura of a deluxe hotel. Modern in concept and design, still there is a sense of Belle Epoque elegance and refined luxury. Thick velvet curtains hang from 17-foot ceilings, deliciously comfortable couches and chairs invite prolonged conversation, and enormous potted palms add to the grandeur of the spacious surroundings. A monumental clock mounted over the reception desk calls to mind movie images of hotel lobbies of the 1940s. Garbo and Crawford would be right at home here.

Off the lobby are two favorite Soho destinations of New Yorkers and visitors alike: the Canal House restaurant, a recipient of glowing reviews from the city's foremost restaurant critics, and the Grand Bar, which offers just-right martinis and flutes of champagne.

Upstairs, the guest rooms continue the stylish acknowledgement of Soho's industrial past and art world present.

Custom-designed desks with glass over chicken wire tops are reminiscent of drafting tables, and the bedside tables resemble sculptors' stands. Frette bed linens, leather headboards, and Kiehl's toiletries are welcome touches in these extremely small rooms. Bathrooms are like those in New York's wonderful old apartment houses, with pedestal sinks, walls of shiny white rectangular tile, and lights that are copied from the gaslights that once lined the streets.

The hotel's location at the southernmost border of Soho makes it ideal for those wanting to explore Chinatown and Little Italy, too, and some of the city's best bargains can be found along bustling Canal Street.

So if downtown is your destination, and proximity to the cutting-edge shops, galleries, and restaurants of Soho a priority, then a stay at the Soho Grand is in order. Stylish, hip, and chic, it takes inspiration from its vibrant surrounding neighborhood, yielding Soho-like results that are particularly Grand.

GUEST SERVICES: Bar on premises; fitness center; laundry services; minibar; parking; room service.

NEIGHBORHOOD RESTAURANTS: Lucky Strike, 59 Grand St. bet. West Broadway and Wooster St., 941-0772 (trendy local bistro with good eclectic menu); Cafe Noir, 32 Grand St. at Thompson St., 431-7910 (French/Moroccan bistro and bar); Nancy Whiskey Pub, 1 Lispenard St. at West Broadway, 226-9943 (neighborhood pub with basic food and fun crowd).

Surrey Hotel

20 East 76th Street bet. Fifth and Madison Avenues
Phone: (212) 288-3700 Fax: (212) 628-1549
Number of Rooms: 130
Price Range: $325 (studio suite)
Credit Cards: All major
www.mesuite.com

THE QUIET, COSMOPOLITAN, EUROPEAN-STYLE
Surrey Hotel is just off Fifth Avenue on New York's Upper
East Side. It's around the corner from the Carlyle and Mark
hotels and a short walk from the Metropolitan, Whitney, and
Frick museums. The Surrey
conveys an understated elegance, attracting an international guest registry: rich,
well-heeled Europeans, art
dealers conducting business
with the Met, and royal families, too; all call the Surrey
home when in New York. This
is a word-of-mouth hotel,
where guests come back again
and again. Where else, after all,
can you get room service from
Cafe Boulud, one of New
York's top restaurants?

Furnished in classic English style, the rooms are light,
cheery, and spacious and include fully equipped kitchens
complete with microwaves. Sparkling marble bathrooms
offer all the amenities including Caswell & Massey toiletries
and thick fluffy towels. Grocery shopping, too, can be
arranged while you're out visiting the many nearby art galleries, museums, antiques stores, and designer clothing boutiques. (Ralph Lauren is only four blocks down Madison
Avenue.) The hotel staff is impeccably professional: Walk
through the lobby and you hear their attention to service.

"Oolong tea for the lady on the sixth floor, coming in from India." "Italian espresso and sparkling water for the family on twelve." And small pets are allowed, an uncommon accommodation at most New York hotels.

Staying at the Surrey is a wonderful old-world experience that puts you in the heart of New York's most affluent neighborhood. With Central Park on one side and the tony strip of upper Madison Avenue on the other side, this is the New York of chauffeur-driven Mercedes, bespoke suits, and ladies who lunch. The Surrey attracts the affluent who don't need to stay at the Carlyle but nevertheless want to stay in this neighborhood. They get everything they want at the Surrey. And you will, too.

GUEST SERVICES: Fitness center; hair dryer; kitchen facilities; restaurant; room service; TV with VCR.
NEIGHBORHOOD RESTAURANTS: Cafe Boulud, 20 East 76th St. bet. 5th and Madison Aves., 772-2600 (one of New York's great restaurants); Coco Pazzo, 23 East 74th St. bet. 5th and Madison Aves., 794-0205 (trendy Italian with excellent food and wines).

Hotel 31

120 East 31st Street bet. Lexington and Park Avenues
Phone: (212) 685-3060 Fax: (212) 532-1232
Number of Rooms: 90
Price Range: Single, $78; double, $110
Credit Cards: None
www.hotel31.com

WHERE FUNKY MEETS RESPECTABLE. Straight from the pages of *Paper* magazine comes the hip-hop hotel of the '90s for the cool budget-conscious traveler. Hotel 31 offers not only style, but also safety, security, cleanliness, and decent-sized rooms at remarkably low rates.

The rooms are smallish, but newly renovated and comfortable. Handsome wood detailing runs along the doors and molding. The new furniture is of dark-stained wood and is quite attractive. Noise levels are surprisingly low, and many of the rooms have sunny views of the surrounding buildings. Absolutely everything is spotless. Of course, at such prices, amenities are few, but it is still a welcome find for the budget-conscious.

Hotel 31 is ideal for a young, hip crowd looking for affordability, cleanliness, and security. Its location is rather nondescript, but it is relatively close by taxi to Midtown and Greenwich Village. Hotel 31 possesses its own idiosyncratic charms, making it a likable choice and worthy destination.

NEIGHBORHOOD RESTAURANTS: Moonstruck Diner, 449 3rd Ave. at 31st St., 213-1100 (Greek diner food); Minar, 95 W. 31st St. at 5th Ave. and Broadway, 967-2727 (good, cheap Indian restaurant); Empire Korea, 6 E. 32nd St. bet. 5th and Madison Aves., 725-1333 (one of the biggest Korean restaurants in town).

Thirty Thirty

30 East 30th Street bet. Park and Madison Avenues
Phone: (212) 689-1900 Fax: (212) 689-0023
Number of Rooms: 230
Price Range: $125–$225
Credit Cards: All major
www.thirtythirty-nyc.com

THIS IS A SLEEK HOTEL WITH UPSCALE AMBITIONS that caters to the budget-minded traveler in the arts and new media. Clean, comfortable rooms offer basic amenities. Black-and-white photos of New York serve as the principal decorating motif. A few blocks from the Empire State Building and just minutes from Chelsea, Midtown, and Gramercy Park, the "Thrifty Thrifty," as it is also known, offers newly minted, affordably priced accommodations in a vibrant, evolving neighborhood.

GUEST SERVICES: TV; daily maid service.
NEIGHBORHOOD RESTAURANTS: Les Halles, 411 Park Ave. S. bet. 28th and 29th Sts., 679-4111 (always-crowded dark French bistro); Mi, 66 Madison Ave. between 27th and 28th Sts., 252-8888 (fusion of the cuisines of Malaysia, Japan, and Thailand); Pump, 113 E. 31st St. between Park and Lexington Aves., 213-5733 (takeout joint specializing in high-protein grub).

The Time

224 West 49th Street bet. Broadway and Eighth Avenue
Phone: (212) 320-2925; 246-5252
Fax: (212) 320-2926; reservations: 1-877-TIME NYC
Number of Rooms: 164 rooms; 28 suites
Price Range: Single, $165; deluxe, $195; penthouse, $1100
Credit Cards: All major
www.thetimeny.com

THE TIME WAS one of the most publicized, new luxury boutique hotels when it opened in 1999, capturing the spirit and creativity of the Times Square renaissance. Designed by interior design czar Adam D. Tihany, the hotel creates an atmosphere that soothes as well as stimulates. A glass-enclosed elevator takes you to the second-floor lobby from the ground-floor arrival area. Primary colors set against the soothing backdrop of taupes and grays create an atmosphere of peace and happiness. At check-in, guests can choose their room's color scheme depending on their mood: blue for tranquility, yellow for happiness, and red to get you hot. Fruits or vegetables in that color adorn the room, along with a booklet explaining the psychological impact of the color. A vial of scent to evoke your selection is also included with your room's many amenities. The Time is a hotel that pays attention to your senses as well as your state of well-being.

Rooms are spacious with high-tech furnishings. Bedspreads and headboards echo your color choice and the imaginative lighting creates a luminous glow at night. Double-paned windows ensure peace and quiet in an otherwise noisy part of town. Televisions are covered in designer canvas so as not to disturb the overall harmony and Zen-like mood of the room. This may be Times Square, but it feels like heaven.

The hotel's bar has become a must for a pre- or post-theater cocktail. The Time's location and innovative approach to guest services make it stylish, charming, and fun. Book a room here on your next visit to experience what everyone is talking about.

GUEST SERVICES: Bar on premises; exercise room; laundry service; restaurant; room service; Web TV; in-room movies. NEIGHBORHOOD RESTAURANTS: Coco Pazzo Teatro, 224 W. 49th St. bet. Broadway and 8th Ave. 320-2929 (Italian food); Iroha, 152 W. 49th St. bet. 6th and 7th Aves., 398-9049 (decent Japanese).

Tribeca Grand Hotel

2 Sixth Avenue bet. White and Walker Streets
Phone: (212) 519-6600 Fax: (212) 519-6700
Number of Rooms: 203, 18 suites
Price Range: $239–$1,600
Credit Cards: All major
www.tribecagrand.com

THIS SELF-PROCLAIMED "TOWN SQUARE OF Tribeca" opened in May 2000 just a few blocks south of its sister hotel, the Soho Grand. Drawing its design inspiration from the neighborhood's industrial architecture, the Tribeca Grand blends the Cast Iron age with 21st-century chic. Wall Streeters, local artists, and prowling hipsters gather under the soaring eight-story atrium and in the adjoining Church Street Lounge (where dogs are welcome) to sip and schmooze in designed and sofa-ed luxury. Steel-caged glass elevators whoosh guests to their rooms. Late-night revelers on their way to Nobu glide by jet-lagged designers just in from Milan. A stylish and dramatic crossroads in the heart of New York's coolest neighborhood.

GUEST SERVICES: Room service; 24-hour fitness center; Internet access.

NEIGHBORHOOD RESTAURANTS: Arqua, 281 Church St. at White St., 334-1888 (authentic Venetian in a civilized setting); El Teddy's, 219 W. Broadway between Franklin and White Sts., 941-7070 (happening Tex-Mex eatery).

W New York

541 Lexington Avenue bet. 49th and 50th Streets
Phone: (212) 755-1200 Fax: (212) 319-8344
Number of Rooms: 720, including 50 suites
Price Range: Standard rooms, $239–$485;
business-class rooms, $279–$525;
standard suites, $329–$575; deluxe suites, $389–$635;
duplex suites, $900; penthouse suites, $1,100
Credit Cards: All major
www.whotels.com

IMAGINE A MONDRIAN PAINTING as a living space. The W New York, one of New York's newest, most exciting, and original boutique hotels, embodies the spirit of the millennium. Part spa, part urban sanctuary, and full of whimsical energy and décor, the W New York propels the concept of lodging into the 21st century.

Messages extolling the W's philosophy greet you everywhere: "Dream with lucidity," "Dance with abandon," "Laugh with gaiety," and "Sleep with angels" can be found on banners festooned from the lobby ceiling or woven into your duvet cover. Poetry for a new age. The public rooms pay homage to nature like water, air, and the canyon. A soothing waterfall cascades in the lobby. Rough-hewn wood-block tables double as backgammon and chessboards. The W is a hotel where the natural world has been brought indoors to serve as a source of solace, calm, and beauty.

The W offers sensory and sensual stimulation at every turn. This way to the juice bar for the macrobiotically inclined—and that way to Rande Gerber's Whiskey Blue,

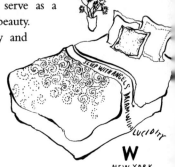

W
NEW YORK

one of the city's hottest night spots. Or over there to Heartbeat, the highly rated restaurant opened by famed restaurateur Drew Nieporent. And no simple lobby concierge here, it's the "Whatever, Whenever" Department. Up on the fourth floor, the Asian-influenced Away spa ascribes to holistic Ayurvedic principles, offering a wide range of body treatments from Pranic healing and color therapy to its signature Star of India warm-oil-drip treatment, all among teak, bamboo, and piles of smooth basalt rocks. The W is a crossroads of desire and fulfillment, a grand hotel for the post-X generation.

Who wants to sleep with so much going on downstairs? But the spirit continues in the upstairs rooms, which are suffused with such life and possibility you tend to overlook the lack of extra leg room and closet space. Resting on your windowsill is the hotel's trademark box of grass—your own soothing little Japanese garden, bringing nature into the bedroom. Designer holes in the headboards give you a Peeping Tom's view of the room, while enhancing the illusion of space. That's the modus operandi here: take necessity and make it fun.

GUEST SERVICES: Bars on-site; fitness center and spa; minibar; restaurant; room service; Web TV and in-room movies. NEIGHBORHOOD RESTAURANTS: Heartbeat, 149 E. 49th St. at Lexington Ave. 407-2900 (organic fare in stunning hotel space); San Martin, 143 E. 49th St. at Lexington Ave., 832-9270 (solid Italian and Spanish cuisine); Diwan Grill, 148 E. 48th St. at Lexington Ave., 593-5425 (elegant regional Indian).

W Court

130 East 39th Street bet. Park and Lexington Avenues
Phone: (212) 592-8832 Fax: (212) 779-8590
Number of Rooms: 198 rooms, 40 suites
Price Range: Double, $209–$345; suites, $299–$435
Credit Cards: All major
www.whotels.com

W Tuscany

120 East 39th Street bet. Park and Lexington Avenues
Phone: (212) 592-8832 Fax: (212) 779-8590
Number of Rooms: 122 rooms
Price range: Double, $219–$300; suites, $309–$390
Credit Cards: All major
www.whotels.com

W HILE THE W NEW YORK SERVES AS THE FLAG-
SHIP of the W Hotel Group in New York, it is the W Court
and W Tuscany that represent the W brand that is being

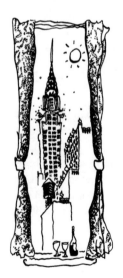

launched around the country. Just a
few doors from one another, these
two properties are operated and
marketed as essentially one hotel
and, along with the W New York,
represent the luxury boutique hotel
of the future.

At the W Court and W Tuscany
you feel as though you are staying in
a friend's stylish New York apartment, designed with contemporary
Banana Republic/Pottery Barn furnishings in rich dark reds and soft
browns. The ebonylike wooden desk
is wide and spacious, and the oversized mirror leaning against the wall
invites self-inspection. Sunlight floods

the space, and the W's signature box of grass adds that essential natural element for tranquility and contemplation.

Downstairs, nightlife pooh-bah Rande Gerber runs the elegant lounge, and celebrity restaurateur Drew Nieporent provides the cuisine and 24-hour room service. The W Court and W Tuscany establish a new standard that all others will be scrambling to keep up with.

GUEST SERVICES: Radio/CD player with extensive CD library; in-room movies; 27-inch TV with Internet access; dual-line cordless phone with speaker and conference capabilities; iron and ironing board; hair dryer; minibar; 24-hour room service; health club; full service spa.

NEIGHBORHOOD RESTAURANTS: Josie's, 561 3rd Ave, at 37th St., 490-1558 (popular Italian eatery with good pastas); Dock's Oyster Bar, 633 3rd Ave. at 40th St., 986-8080 (popular, boisterous seafood grill).

W Times Square

1567 Broadway at 47th Street
Phone: (212) 930-7400 Fax: (212) 930-7500
Number of rooms: 509
Price range: $229 (a wonderful room)–
$339 (a spectacular king)
Credit Cards: All major
www.whotels.com

AS YOU APPROACH THE W TIMES SQUARE from Broadway the anticipation starts to build. You first see the black-uniformed attendants with the hidden earpieces and walkie-talkies. Are these refugees from P. Diddy's posse or ex-operatives from the Secret Service? Pass under the theatrical marquee with the ever-changing blinking, colored lights, and you've entered a waterworld of rushing cascades to the side of you, shimmering pools overhead, and moody techno music all around. Is this the Buddha Lounge or a hotel? Am I on the guest list to this private party? Whoosh upstairs to the seventh-floor lobby and you enter a world of creatively inspired design and comfort with touches of ironic humor sprinkled along the way. This feels like an exclusive club, and you are graciously welcome. Sip a cocktail at one of the canoodling nooks across from the long white bar or lounge on one of the modern couches and take it all in. I couldn't help but laugh at the glittering sequined mannequins lined up along the back wall and posing on the reception desks. This is so New York, so now and so fun. Upstairs the rooms are decorated in soothing browns and grays and offer all the latest creature comforts. Book a room overlooking Times Square or out over the Hudson River. Mine looked out over the Intrepid Sea, Air, and Space Museum and the boats going up and down the river. Don't miss the "Wish" pillow that adorns every bed. To paraphrase Oscar Wilde, no matter what you wish for, the W Times Square has already taken care of it.

The W Times Square, which opened in December of 2001, captures the essence of the energy, pulse, and style of

New York and delivers it to you amidst beautiful modern surroundings, pampering luxury, and all the amenities. And to complement all this, the staff is extremely friendly and helpful—no attitude here. For the ultra–New York experience in the ultra–New York location, book a room at the W Times Square the next time you are in town.

GUEST SERVICES: 24 hour room service; on-site fitness center; business center.

NEIGHBORHOOD RESTAURANTS: Dervish, 146 W. 47th St. between 6th and 7th Aves., 997-0070 (tasty Turkish fare in a classic Broadway haunt setting); Edison Café, 228 W 47th St. between Broadway and 8th Ave., 354-0368 (popular coffee shop in the Edison Hotel); Meskerem, 468 W. 47th St. between 9th and 10th Aves., 664-0520 (fun, inexpensive Ethiopian spot where no cutlery is used).

W Union Square

201 Park Avenue South at 17th Street
Phone: (212) 253-9119 Fax: (212) 253-9229
Number of Rooms: 270; 17 suites including 1 Presidential suite
Price Range: $289–$899, Presidential suite $1,800
Credit Cards: All major
www.whotels.com

THIS RECENT ADDITION to the rapidly expanding W boutique hotel chain opened its doors in November 2000. Located in the former beaux-arts-style Guardian Life Building overlooking Union Square Park, this is a quintessential downtown hotel, as chic and fashionable as the cool, young, well-heeled hipsters who stay and work there. Walk through the lobby and all the signs are evident: beeping cell phones, clicking palm pilots, de rigueur black leather, the latest accessories from Sigerson Morrison, and conversations tinged with international accents. Squeeze yourself into the always happening Underbar brought to you by nightlife maven Rande Gerber. Or sample the highly acclaimed rustic fare of superstar chef Todd English at Olives, the hotel's excellent restaurant. The W is a destination hotel for so many reasons.

GUEST SERVICES: 24-hour room service; health spa and fitness center.

NEIGHBORHOOD RESTAURANTS: Zen Palate, 34 Union Square E. at 16th St., 614-9345 (trendy yet soothing vegetarian spot); Coffee Shop, 29 Union Square W. at 16th St., 243-7969 (large, hip café with Brazilian-American fare); Republic, 37 Union Square W. at 17th St., 627-7172 (large, happening, always-crowded Asian that's cheap and cheery).

146 BEST LITTLE HOTELS

Hotel Wales

1295 Madison Avenue at 92nd Street
Phone: (212) 876-6000 Fax: (212) 860-7000
Number of Rooms: 92 (47 suites)
Price Range: Single or double, $209; suite, $335
Credit Cards: All major
www.waleshotel.com

YOU MAY FIND YOURSELF thinking you've been transported to an inn in London's Knightsbridge when you enter
the hushed, intimate lobby of the Hotel Wales. Decorated
with striped wallpaper in two shades of green and wood
paneling, the space is accented by leather armchairs, original
watercolors from Alain Vaes's *Puss in Boots*, leather-bound
volumes of *Country Life*, and a Bach concerto on the sound
system. In fact, an Edwardian/Victorian sensibility and a love
of classical music pervade every nook of this charming boutique hotel on the Upper East Side. Each morning at 8 A.M.
a harpist entertains during tea in the second-floor Pied Piper
Room, a period salon with antique furnishings and Oriental
carpets gracing the oak wood floors.

Guest rooms have been recently renovated, many featuring intricate oak woodwork, fireplaces, marble sinks with
brass fixtures, and pleasant city views. (Ask for a room over-
looking Central Park with a wonderful view of the reservoir.
Lines 01 and 19 are the sunniest.) Furnishings are antique-
like and the beds feature off-white linen bedspreads and
fluffy down pillows. The smallish bathrooms are tidy and
functional. The hotel's vast CD library emphasizes
Beethoven and Mozart but also includes classic jazz, and the
video collection tends to well-known independent and art-
house titles. For opera aficionados there are full stereo videos
of every 1995–1996 Metropolitan Opera production.

Although the hotel's Carnegie Hill location makes it a
six-dollar cab ride to Midtown, and the East Side Lexington
Avenue subway line is a ten-minute walk away, the surrounding neighborhood has plenty to offer in the way of elegant

shops, restaurants, and coffee bars. What better way to escape
the maddening crowd than to stroll one block to Central Park
and take a morning amble around the one-and-a-half mile
jogging track circling the reservoir.

The Wales has that wonderful feel of a quiet romantic
country inn where personal attention is paid to the important details that really matter to a guest, yet it's only minutes
from the city's hustle and bustle. The Wales provides the hush
one needs to face the rush.

GUEST SERVICES: Complimentary breakfast and cappuccino;
CD player; CD, video, and book library; restaurant; fitness-
center/spa; room service; Internet access; TV; valet parking.
NEIGHBORHOOD RESTAURANTS: Sarabeth's, 1295 Madison
Ave. bet. 92nd and 93rd Sts., 410-7335 (American country-
cooking, best for brunch); Island, 1305 Madison Ave. bet.
92nd and 93rd Sts., 996-1200 (northern Italian-French fare
in fun preppy setting).

Wall Street Inn

9 South William Street (at Broad Street)
Phone: (212) 747-1500 Fax: (212) 747-1900
Number of Rooms: 46
Price Range: $169–$249
Credit Cards: All major
www.thewallstreetinn.com
manager@thewallstreetinn.com

ON A NARROW SIDE STREET just steps from the New York Stock Exchange stands the former headquarters of Lehman Brothers investment bank that, in August of 1999, was converted into this charming boutique hotel. Step through its formidable doors and you are immediately transported from the canyons of the Financial District to Colonial Williamsburg. Upholstered chairs and sofas, mahogany paneling, and patchwork quilts evoke the feel of a country bed and breakfast. Personal touches, like fresh flowers and plants in the room, give this inn a "home away from home" feel. Who says Wall Street can't be warm and welcoming?

GUEST SERVICES: Continental breakfast; fitness center with sauna and steam room.

NEIGHBORHOOD RESTAURANTS: Delmonico's, 56 Beaver St. at South William, 509-1144 (upscale, classic American); Beckett's Bar and Grill, 78 Pearl St. at Broad St., 269-1001 (good, popular after-work bar).

Washington Square Hotel

103 Waverly Place at MacDougal Street
Phone: (212) 777-9515 (212) 979-8373
Number of Rooms: 163
Price Range: Single, $116–$136; quad, $167–$190
Credit Cards: All major
www.washingtonsquarehotel.com

IN THE CENTER OF GREENWICH VILLAGE, over-looking the always lively and interesting Washington Square Park, is the quirky Washington Square Hotel. Home to New York University and the setting for much of New York's early history and culture, this part of the city is enticing both for its youthful energy and its rich architectural heritage. A walk to the famous arch and along Washington Square North can almost transport you into a Henry James novel.

The dearth of hotels in this part of downtown makes this an obvious choice for those wanting to stay in the heart of the Village. It's one of those places that New Yorkers always ask about. "How is that place? Didn't they just renovate it a few years back?" Everyone seems eager to recommend it to visiting friends.

Several years ago, a $10 million renovation was completed to bring this hotel into the 21st century. The elegant lobby with its Italian marble floor, wrought iron gate, and ornithology prints promises a charming ambiance. While these promises aren't entirely fulfilled, the upstairs rooms are cozy and clean, though small, with modest furnishings. Sixty of the 163 rooms offer views of the park, generally a plus if you don't mind the occasionally high noise level.

Breakfast is served in the lobby's popular North Square restaurant, which also offers good American bistro fare in a lovely setting at lunch and dinner.

While the Washington Square Hotel may not be a sweet boutique hotel, it does possess a certain Parisian Left Bank charm. Its reasonable rates and excellent location definitely make it worth a try. So bring along a Henry James novel, mingle with the students browsing the used book tables on West 4th Street, and take in some neighborhood jazz—all experiences that will make you glad you decided to stay in the Village.

GUEST SERVICES: Complimentary continental breakfast; fitness center; restaurant with bar.

NEIGHBORHOOD RESTAURANTS: Minetta Tavern, 113 MacDougal St. bet. W. 3rd and Bleecker Sts., 475-3850 (quintessential Village Italian restaurant); Baluchi's, 361 6th Ave. at Washington Place, 929-2441 (elegant Indian restaurant with reasonable prices); Gray's Papaya, 402 6th Ave. at 8th St., 260-3532 (one of the great cheap eats in town).

15 More Best Little Hotels . . .

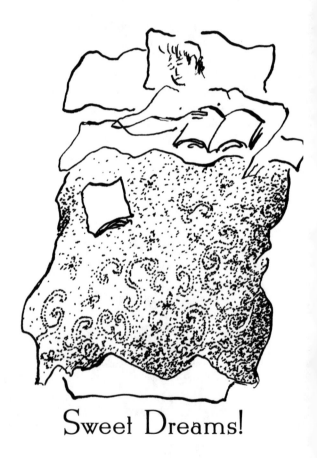

Sweet Dreams!

AMERITANIA HOTEL 54
230 West 54th Street bet. Broadway and Eighth Ave.
Phone: (212) 247-5000 Fax: (212) 247-3316
Reservations: (800) 922-0330
Price Range: Standard room, $195–$245; suite, $285–$595
No. of Rooms: 207, 12 suites Credit Cards: All major
www.nychotels.com

This pleasant little hotel on the northern reaches of the Times Square area is within walking distance of the Theater District, Midtown, and Central Park. Newly renovated; up-to-the-minute features; average-size rooms; clean, sleek, stylized modern interior; helpful staff. A delightful choice.

AMSTERDAM COURT
226 West 50th Street bet. Broadway and Eighth Ave.
Phone: (212) 459-1000 Fax: (212) 265-5070
Price Range: Standard, $165; suite, $250
No. of Rooms: 117 Credit Cards: All major
www.nychotels.com

A modest yet stylish little hotel in the Theater District where the service is especially friendly. All the rooms, although small, are decorated nicely with contemporary furnishings. Be sure to check out the new roof deck.

THE CARNEGIE HOTEL
229 West 58th Street bet. Broadway and Seventh Ave.
Phone: (212) 245-4000 Fax: (212) 245-6199
Reservations: (800) 964-6835
Price Range: Double, $250–$350
No. of Rooms: 20 Credit Cards: All major
www.newyorkhotel.com

This quiet hotel is right around the corner from Carnegie Hall, one block from Central Park, and a brisk walk to Midtown, the Theater District, or Lincoln Center. Tastefully decorated, every room includes a kitchenette and numerous amenities, including a 25-inch television. The lobby is bright and comfortable.

COMFORT INN CENTRAL PARK WEST HOTEL
31 West 71st Street bet. Central Park West and Columbus Ave.
Phone: (212) 721-4770 Fax: (212) 579-8544
Price Range: $99–$259
No. of Rooms: 94 Credit Cards: All major
www.comfortinn.com/hotel/ny209

Formerly the Hampshire Central Park, this Euro-style boutique hotel, located in a lively residential neighborhood, is a good choice for a business and leisure travelers. Among the amenities, a complimentary, deluxe continental breakfast and exercise room. Minutes from Lincoln Center and theaters.

DORAL PARK AVENUE
70 Park Avenue at 38th St.
Phone: (212) 687-7050 Fax: (212) 949-5924
Price Range: $185–400
No. of Rooms: 188, 14 suites Credit Cards: All major
www.doralparkavenue.com

This traditional European-style hotel offers good value for the money. Spacious, comfortable rooms in quiet Murray Hill location near Midtown. With room service and use of fitness center.

EAST VILLAGE BED AND COFFEE
110 Avenue C bet. Seventh and Eighth Sts.
Phone/Fax: (212) 533-4175
Price Range: Single, $65–$70; Double, $75–$85
No. of Rooms: 6 Credit Cards: All major
www.bedandcoffee.com

If you're on a limited budget and would enjoy staying in Alphabet City in the East Village, here's an option. The six guest rooms are simple but comfortable and share a kitchen and living area. The owner, Carlos Delfin, lives here with his dog, Frong. Don't be put off by the graffiti-strewn entrance—it's part of the local color.

THE ELLINGTON
610 West 111th Street bet. Broadway and Riverside Drive
Phone: (212) 864-7500 Fax: (212) 749-5852

Price Range: Single, $125; double, $165
No. of Rooms: 81   Credit Cards: All major

Looking for affordable accommodations way uptown? This 81-room six-story budget hotel was completely renovated in late 1998. Rooms are decorated in modern black and white and have brass beds, TVs, and telephones. Steps from Riverside Park and a short walk to Columbia University.

HOTEL 17

225 East 17th Street bet. Third and Second Aves.
Phone: (212) 475-2845   Fax: (212) 677-8178
Price Range: Single, $75; triple, $200
No. of Rooms: 130
Credit Cards: None; cash or travelers checks only
www.hotel17ny.com

Located on a brownstone-lined block near Gramercy Park, Hotel 17 is best for the younger set when the Gershwin is full. The funky clientele, eclectic furnishings, and limited amenities give the place its own distinct character.

MARCEL HOTEL

201 East 24th Street bet. Second and Third Aves.
Phone: (212) 696-3800   Fax: (212) 696-0077
Price Range: $185–$250
No. of Rooms: 100   Credit Cards: All major
www.nychotels.com

Another well-priced little hotel near Gramercy Park. Rooms decorated with flair have VCRs, CD players, and data port telephones. Home of the trendy new Spread restaurant, with many other such hot spots nearby on Park Avenue South. Try to book a room facing 24th Street, as Third Avenue is noisy.

THE MAYFAIR NEW YORK

242 West 49th Street bet. Broadway and Eighth Ave.
Phone: (212) 586-0300   Fax: (212) 307-5226
Reservations: (800) 556-2932
Price Range: Single, $90–$190; double, $110–$290
No. of Rooms: 78   Credit Cards: All major

Located in the heart of the Theater District, this delightful

European-style hotel caters to a crowd of business and leisure travelers. Renovated in 1997, there is an ambiance of taste, refinement, and old-world style. Check out the hotel's new Garrick restaurant, a handsome bistro with classic French dishes.

THE MODERNE

243 West 55th Street bet. Broadway and Eighth Ave.
Phone: (212) 397-6767 Fax: (212) 397-8787
Price Range: Single, $130–$175; suite, $205
No. of Rooms: 37 Credit Cards: All major
www.nychotels.com

This nice little hotel offers modest, newly renovated rooms with a little panache (an Andy Warhol "Marilyn" print hangs in every room). There's a small lobby and a breakfast room on the second floor. Just a little west of everything you could possibly want to see and do in Midtown.

ON THE AVE HOTEL

2178 Broadway at 77th St.
Phone: (212) 362-1100 Fax: (212) 787-9521
Reservations: (800) 497-6028
Price Range: Standard, $175; deluxe, $215; penthouses, $350
No. of Rooms: 250 Credit Cards: All major
www.STAYinNY.com

This affordable West Side hotel has modern, comfortable rooms that feature "floating beds." Near Central Park, Lincoln Center, great restaurants, bars, clubs, and shops.

PORTLAND SQUARE HOTEL

132 West 47th Street bet. Broadway and Sixth Ave.
Phone: (212) 382-0600 Fax: (212) 382-0684
Reservations: (800) 388-8988
Price Range: Single, $65; triple, $150
No. of Rooms: 149 Credit Cards: All major
www.portlandsquarehotel.com

Jimmy Cagney once lived at this Times Square hotel and he remains its claim to fame. Answering the needs of the budget traveler who wants to be in the center of New York, the Portland Square is clean, cheap, and neat. Rooms are small, many with shared bath. Temper your expectations and get good value for your money.

SECOND HOME ON SECOND AVENUE
221 Second Avenue bet. 13th and 14th Sts.
Phone/Fax: (212) 677-3161
Price Range: Single, $60; suite, $155
No. of Rooms: 7   Credit Cards: All major
www.secondhome.citysearch.com

If you want to stay in the East Village, this is a gem. Each of the seven rooms is tastefully decorated in a different theme (Caribbean, Tribal, etc.) and offers TV, VCR, and a fully stocked kitchen. Rooms and closets are large, but note that the building has four floors and no elevator.

URBAN JEM GUESTHOUSE
2005 Fifth Avenue bet. 124th and 125th Sts.
Phone: (212) 831-6029   Fax: (212) 831-6940
Price Range: Single, $100; suite, $220
No. of Rooms: 4   Credit Cards: All major
www.urbanjem.com

A charming bed and breakfast in a brownstone in the Mount Morris Park Historic District of Harlem. Owned and operated by Jane Alex Mendelson, the guest house is decorated with paintings by several artists, including Mendelson. Rooms have television/telephone; two have private bath and kitchen and two share a bath and kitchen.

INDEX BY NEIGHBORHOOD

About the Author

Allen Sperry is president of Manhattan Intelligence (www.manhattani.com), a research firm specializing in New York-based information. He is a regular on *The WOR Morning Show*, where he gives "The Intelligence Report." A graduate of the Harvard Business School, Allen lives in New York with his wife and two children.

About the Artist

With his folding chair, sketchbook, and bottle of ink, John Coburn is happiest working on location. He exhibits in New York and Toronto, where he lives with his wife Leslie and their two children. He is represented by Beckett Fine Art. John also did the drawings for *New York's 50 Best Places to Discover and Enjoy in Central Park*.